Risk-Mapping and Local Capacities:
Lessons from Mexico and
Central America

Monica Trujillo

Amado Ordóñez

Carlos Hernández

Oxfam

Available from Bournemouth English Book Centre, PO Box 1496, Parkstone, Dorset, BH12 3YD, UK
tel: +44 (0)1202 712933; fax: +44 (0)1202 712930; email: oxfam@bebc.co.uk.

and from the following agents:
USA: Stylus Publishing LLC, PO Box 605, Herndon, VA 20172-0605, USA
tel: +1 (0)703 661 1581; fax: +1 (0)703 661 1547; email: styluspub@aol.com

Southern Africa: David Philip Publishers, PO Box 23408, Claremont 7735, South Africa
tel: +27 (0)21 674 4136; fax: +27 (0)21 674 3358; email: orders@dpp.co.za

For details of local agents and representatives in other countries, consult our website:
http://www.oxfam.org.uk/publications.html
or contact Oxfam Publishing, 274 Banbury Road, Oxford OX2 7DZ, UK
tel. +44 (0)1865 311 311; fax +44 (0)1865 312 600; email publish@oxfam.org.uk.

Printed by Oxfam Print Room

Oxfam GB is a registered charity, no. 202 918, and is a member of Oxfam International.

Contents

3

Acknowledgements

The following people were involved in this exercise: two consultants from Mexico and Central America; a specialist from the Emergencies Department of Oxfam GB, and staff from Oxfam's offices in the region. Leaders of indigenous, *campesino*, and women's organisations in the region contributed their knowledge and grassroots experience during the visits to high-risk communities. Representatives from a range of government bodies and civil-society organisations also participated as interviewees.

The original report was published by Oxfam in Nicaragua in 1999 under the title *Mapeo de Riesgos y Vulnerabilidad en Centroamerica y México: Estudio de capacidades locales para trabajar en situaciones de emergencía* (copies available free of charge from Oxfam Regional Office, Altamira D. Esté, Casa 322 y 323, Managua, email: oxfam@oxcamex.org.ni). It was translated from Spanish by Sophie Bond, Caroline Fox, and Claire Idle. It was edited and adapted for publication as an Oxfam Working Paper by Deborah Eade.

Abbreviations and acronyms

ALIDES — Central American Alliance for Sustainable Development

CENAPRED — National Centre for the Prevention of Disasters (Mexico)

CEPREDENAC — Co-ordinating Centre for the Prevention of Natural Disasters in Central America

CEPRODE — Centre for Disaster Protection (El Salvador)

CESCO — Centre for Research and Control of Pollutants (Honduras)

CNE — National Emergencies Commission (Costa Rica)

COCOPA — Peace Conciliation Commission (Mexico)

COEN — National Committee for Emergencies (El Salvador)

CONRED — National Commission for the Reduction of Disasters (Guatemala)

COPECO — Permanent Commission for Contingencies (Honduras)

EMNDC — High Command of National Civil Defence (Nicaragua)

FACS — Augusto César Sandino Foundation (Nicaragua)

FLACSO — Latin American Faculty of Social Sciences

ICRC — International Committee of the Red Cross

IDRND — International Decade for the Reduction of Natural Disasters

IFRCS — International Federation of Red Cross/Red Crescent Societies

INSIVUMEH — National Institute of Seismology, Vulcanology, Meteorology, and Hydrology (Guatemala)

ITCZ — Intertropical Convergence Zone

LA RED — Network of Social Studies for the Prevention of Natural Disasters in Latin America

MSF — Médecins Sans Frontières

OAS — Organisation of American States

OFDA — US Office for Disaster Response

PAHO — Pan-American Health Organisation (Organización Panamericana de la Salud, OPS)

SARH — Department of Agriculture and Water Resources (Mexico)

SINAPROC — National System for Civil Protection (Mexico)

SINRED — National System for the Reduction of Disasters (Guatemala)

UNAM — Autonomous University of Mexico (UNAM)

Preface

In March 1997 a multidisciplinary team was commissioned by Oxfam GB to identify the risks of disasters — whether of natural origin or human agency — throughout Mexico and Central America. Their findings, reported in this Working Paper, demonstrated the urgent need to find ways to reduce the degree of vulnerability faced by many urban and rural communities in the region. It was initially hoped that it would be possible to set out the framework for a Disaster Preparedness Plan which, along with the development programmes that Oxfam GB was supporting, would help to articulate the research team's vision of reshaping and uniting emergency relief with rehabilitation and development activities.

No one imagined then that the El Niño phenomenon, which brought drought to southern Honduras and western Nicaragua and contributed to the region's greatest recorded loss of woodland through forest fires, would eventually result in the biggest environmental catastrophe in recent years; or that this in turn would lead to the serious questioning of social and economic policies which have been so detrimental to huge numbers of people, particularly indigenous communities, women, and children. But the fact is that Hurricane Mitch, which devastated Central America in November 1998, was not only what the 1999 *World Disasters Report* terms 'a super-disaster'[1] — the third-strongest hurricane of the century — but also an occurrence which magnified the already severe degrees of poverty and vulnerability in the region.

Mitch, which brought to Central America a whole year's rainfall in a few hours, affected the lives of six million people. Between 10,000 and 15,000 people lost their lives and 2.5 million became temporarily dependent upon aid. In Honduras, up to 70 per cent of export crops were lost. Eighty per cent of the country's aqueducts were damaged and thousands of public and domestic sanitation facilities were ruined: some 100,000 latrines were destroyed in the capital alone. In Nicaragua, thousands lost their lives; in addition, five villages were buried in the débris produced by the eruption of the Casitas Volcano. The resulting losses of the two disasters combined were estimated at US$1,500 million, a significant amount for such a fragile economy. Guatemala and El Salvador suffered less damage overall, though the effects were no less serious for the people involved: in El Salvador there were some 85,000 victims, and in Guatemala up to 100,000 people had to be evacuated from their homes. The most severely affected regions were those that had been identified in the Oxfam study as high-risk areas, hit by land-slides in Tegucigalpa and fierce floods in the River Coco and the Sula valley, to name but a few. The longer-term consequences of Mitch have included the outbreak of rat-borne disease in Nicaragua, resulting from contaminated and damaged sanitation systems and exacerbated by inadequate public health provision — something highlighted in the study.

This comprehensive review of the threats and risks of disasters across the region is thus particularly pertinent. Its focus on the links between socio-economic realities, policies, and the dynamics of planning in a context where the limits of vulnerability are essentially a human responsibility is perhaps one of its most important contributions. The maps showing the regional patterns of risk and vulnerability enable us to appreciate the importance of risk management in order to reduce vulnerability and insecurity and achieve sustainable development.

The methodology adopted in the study allows one to map out and evaluate the threats and risks of various kinds of disaster in the region, and can be adapted for use in other settings. The risk of exposure to phenomena such as hurricanes, seismic and volcanic activity, floods, landslides, tidal waves, and droughts is widely recognised; likewise risks and threats that are political in nature, such as the armed conflicts that engulfed much of the region from the 1970s until very recently. Conflicts and social unrest were themselves linked to the widespread insecurity, and these links are explored in the study. Other risks are linked to the environmental crisis, whose effects may be irreversible and may in turn provoke major disasters. Examples include the extensive deforestation of the region, the reduction of water resources, and solid-waste contamination.

Perhaps the most surprising elements of the study, however, concern its depiction of vulnerability on a regional scale. Social, political, and economic realities are intimately linked to the factors that make people more or less vulnerable to risks and threats. In this regard, the need for ordinary women and men to be empowered through enabling them to participate in making decisions concerning their vulnerability is accorded a greater importance than technical considerations. For social vulnerability affects people's living conditions at the local and even the individual or household levels, while these conditions relate to the resources available to a given community and the extent to which they are excluded and marginalised by macro-economic and social policies.

As in development work, it is important to differentiate between the vulnerabilities of men and women, and not fall into the trap of developing emergency responses or disaster-preparedness plans that do not take these differences into account. The study draws particular attention to the implications of female poverty in the region, the huge number of women-maintained households, women's poor health and nutritional status, the low level of female participation in civil society, and other factors that will intensify their vulnerability in emergency situations.

The study shows the critical importance of seeing emergency relief and development work as intimately linked with each other, and not as mutually exclusive. This means that any efforts, at whatever level, to develop social and economic policies should be committed to reducing vulnerability as well as to involving community structures in local-level disaster management. One of the main lessons from the Mitch disaster is that of the need to move towards a culture of disaster preparedness in every sphere, and to create living conditions and promote sustainable development methods that help to reduce vulnerability. In the words of UN Secretary-General Kofi Annan, speaking at the May 1999 donors' meeting in Stockholm:

The unfinished political and human rights agendas of the peace process, and the reconstruction agenda following the loss of life, devastation and ruin brought on by Hurricane Mitch ... are compatible, mutually reinforcing agendas. The two agendas — peace and reconstruction — both address pivotal questions relating to poverty, social inequity, population pressures and environmental sustainability. Both involved crucial issues such as local development, decentralisation, transparency, good governance and institution-building ... We look to donors and international financial institutions to continue their support and to do their utmost for more and quicker debt relief. And we look to the United Nations family to assist governments in ensuring that preparations are in place for the next hurricane season; and to help the countries of the region establish more just societies.[2]

Less than six months after this statement, however, seasonal tropical depressions caused torrential rains in parts of Mexico, resulting in mudslides and floods that killed 400 people and left more than 200,000 homeless in the poorer and more precarious districts of Puebla and Veracruz. The country's civil protection and emergency-response systems were the subject of much public criticism.

In terms of its far-reaching recommendations concerning the links between development, vulnerability, and emergencies — and the implications for aid and co-operation programmes — the risk-mapping exercise represents far more than a report that merely says who does what and with whom in disaster situations. Within Oxfam GB, the overall mapping methodology, with its focus on the regional as well as the local level, has enabled us to target the high-priority areas in terms of their vulnerability to risk and threat. To achieve this, we have given top priority to strengthening local capacities and to re-thinking our assumptions about how to address or pre-empt emergencies through an approach to development which incorporates participation, but which is also aware of the need to differentiate between the various roles of key actors such as the state and civil society.

As the incidence of natural disasters world-wide is increasing, while the structural risks posed by armed conflict, environmental degradation, and pollution show little sign of abating, it is both a great responsibility and an opportunity for international NGOs to foster a culture of disaster preparedness in which preparedness management is seen to be accorded the same priority as other needs and challenges in development, and which thus aims to minimise the vulnerability of the millions of people who are marginalised and socially excluded in Central America and elsewhere.

Adolfo Castrillo
(Former Deputy Regional Representative for Central America and Mexico, Oxfam GB)

Notes

1 The *World Disasters Report 1999* was published by the International Federation of Red Cross and Red Crescent Societies. It stated that natural disasters tripled in the 1990s compared with the 1960s, with more than 700 'large-loss' catastrophes occurring in 1998 alone.

2 Quoted in *Go-Between* 76, August-September 1999, p.27.

1 Introduction

Background to the risk-mapping exercise

Oxfam GB (hereafter referred to as 'Oxfam') has always been involved in a broad range of humanitarian aid programmes. It views emergency relief work as a way of addressing the needs that arise from poverty and suffering, and seeks through its interventions to optimise people's capacity to control the factors that affect them in their daily lives, as well as to influence humanitarian aid policies and practices in a wider context.

Emergencies and natural disasters which interrupt the processes of development, or which exacerbate existing instabilities and/or conflicts, often precipitate a crisis for the poor. In Mexico and Central America, Oxfam has long supported impoverished communities whose lives have been affected by natural phenomena and conflicts. Its aim in these circumstances is to strengthen the capacity of the poor and marginalised to bring about changes which are positive and sustainable, and to reduce their vulnerability in the event of emergencies or any other situations in which their basic rights are denied.

Oxfam's Programme of Preparedness for Emergencies in Mexico and Central America is an essential step towards providing an effective, efficient, and appropriate humanitarian response to emergencies in this region. The mapping exercise that forms the basis of this Working Paper represents a starting point in developing this programme. The mapping exercise had the following aims.

- To predict possible emergencies that might arise in the region and to ascertain their potential impact on those most affected.
- To identify the local capacity for emergency response within each country.
- To envisage the type of external assistance needed for an effective and appropriate response to emergencies.

The exercise began with a literature review, including Oxfam's own policy documents on the subject, in order to establish an institutional framework and to identify existing processes and initiatives within this field. An overall methodology was then agreed as a basis for defining the nature of the risks, vulnerabilities, and capacities in the region; for selecting the indicators and determining the variables and weightings to be used in assessing them; and for formulating tools for gathering, processing, and analysing information. Field visits were made to Costa Rica, El Salvador, and Honduras, using the original methodology. In the second phase, the methodology and criteria used were broader, and visits were made to high-risk areas in Guatemala, Mexico, and Nicaragua. Neither Panama nor Belize was included in the main exercise.

Methodology

It is always a challenge to represent in simple terms the complex reality within which emergency situations occur, in a way that also allows one to visualise the key elements in an aid agency's decision-making process. As a point of departure, we assume that emergencies are not external to the on-going development processes, but are part of them. They constitute interruptions or crises which then have major repercussions on the development opportunities of a given community or area. Since disasters always have the potential to undermine development, measures to prevent, prepare for, and mitigate disasters should inform every plan and strategy for sustainable development.

We assumed that this methodology should be a tool for people who are not disaster experts, but whose depth of local knowledge and experience makes them experts in the conditions and potentialities of a given country, region, or locality. This study thus sought to develop a fuller analysis than one based on technical expertise alone, by combining relevant formal information with the accumulated experience of local actors. Although the methodology was devised to assess risks, vulnerabilities, and local capacities at a regional level, it can also be adapted for local-level application.

The threats to be studied were selected on the basis of the most frequent events or disasters in the region, though some were included because of the severity of their impact, rather than because of their frequency. The scenarios were those most likely to occur in Mexico and Central America, in order to provide a comprehensive view of the region, and the threat or risk of disasters, whether natural or of human agency. Qualitative and quantitative indicators were established. The first phase of the study sought to validate the methodology by testing it against a range of diverse and complex realities. Adjustments were subsequently made to take account of the fact that it was not possible to consult as many people in the region as had been hoped, and because not all the information we had expected to be available was accessible; hence we had to make use of some old data and also abandon some of the proposed indicators. Despite these constraints, we none the less achieved a fairly accurate level of approximation in the first phase of the exercise.

Physical characteristics of the region: an overview

Five tectonic plates meet in the area covered by Mexico and Central America, the movement and interaction of which determine the extremely high seismic activity throughout the region (principally along the Pacific coastline), which causes frequent earthquakes and occasional tsunamis (tidal waves created by quakes on the seabed). There is also an active chain of volcanoes right down the Pacific Strip, with the Tacaná volcano actually linking Mexico with the Central American isthmus. In addition, four cyclogenetic zones are present in the Pacific and the Atlantic ocean masses, in which there is activity throughout the annual hurricane season (June–November).

The prevailing climate patterns, together with ecological deterioration, are resulting in irregular and changing rainfall patterns, which subject wide areas to a continuous fluctuation between increasingly severe floods and droughts. Other phenomena, such as earthquakes or tornadoes, affect only a limited area, but have a significant impact.

The region's economic structure is dependent on international markets and powers, with regard both to the sale of products (mainly agricultural) and the acquisition of raw materials and technology for the manufacture of basic goods. In general, wealth is highly concentrated among small, prosperous minorities who co-exist with a marginalised and growing majority who live in extreme poverty. A fairly uniform economic structural adjustment model has been applied throughout the region over the last decade. Although this has led to an apparent improvement in macro-economic performance, there has also been rising unemployment, a depression in agricultural production (principally affecting *campesino* [peasant] producers and the indigenous peoples), and a widening gap between rich and poor.

The structural adjustment packages have also resulted in widespread cuts in basic services in the areas of health-care services, education, welfare services, and housing. Deepening poverty and widespread social exclusion have frequently resulted in the population of whole areas being marginalised. The most deprived areas and social sectors are also those most at risk from disasters of all kinds, a fact which in turn makes them more vulnerable still.

With the exception of Costa Rica, all of the countries in the region are now at a crucial point in their political history, in that they are all in an immediate post-war phase, or are currently experiencing armed conflicts. The processes of setting up institutions and mechanisms for democratic participation are still in their infancy. There is also great uncertainty, generated by a high degree of economic and social polarisation, and popular distrust of public bodies and political parties which have proved unable to rise above sectarianism, making it difficult to reach a consensus or to prioritise national interests.

Outline of contents

The **analysis of threats** establishes the incidence and distribution of threats present in the region, and the particularities of each country with respect to probability, intensity, and area covered. The sectors and elements exposed to the threat are then analysed, in particular the threatened communities, agro-ecological conditions and the state of the economy, infrastructure, and services (**risk analysis**). This is followed by an **analysis of vulnerability**, defined as the relationship between the level of risk, local capacities, and the living conditions of the threatened community. The level of vulnerability can be modified according to certain trace indicators, including the capacity to predict occurrences, communication systems, the capacity of health-care systems, general levels of education, and levels of disease. A risk map also considers the wider factors that determine the conditions in which such communities live.

The risk map undertakes an **analysis of local capacities,** by considering firstly the institutional framework for the management of disasters, regionally, nationally, and locally. Secondly, it assesses current capacities from the perspective of civil society. Finally, it considers initiatives for developing existing capacities, and the principal actors who have a role to play in this. It identifies steps already taken, and current shortcomings in the fields of prevention, preparedness, rehabilitation, and response; and then assesses these and establishes a framework for future priorities. Factors that indicate specific capacities are, among others, those related to the management of information regarding disasters: analysis and evaluation of the context and environment, co-ordination, and operational and management plans for working in emergencies.

An in-depth study of the current situation formed part of the risk map, but is presented only in summary form in this Working Paper since, by its very nature, such information is liable to change in a relatively short time. The focus here is on the capacity of institutions to tackle emergency situations in their different shapes and forms, identifying the strengths and weaknesses of the key players in the region in the detection, diagnosis, planning, intervention, and evaluation of emergencies. This paper also considers emergencies in the context of development and establishes immediate and future challenges for work in the region.

The **conclusions** include an evaluation of disasters in the region, assessing progress and shortcomings in the fields of prevention, preparedness, mitigation, response, and restoration. This final section attempts to identify the principal players in the context of disasters in the region, and makes recommendations for likely scenarios.

2 Assessment of threats and risks

Identification and analysis of threats

In Central America, most natural phenomena that cause disasters are already well understood, and great advances have also been made in Mexico. However, regarding the phenomena associated with seismic activity there remain some unstudied areas (principally in Central America). The potential for seismic activity along the Pacific coasts has been comprehensively studied, but there is as yet no seismo-tectonic model to explain events of recent years along the Atlantic coastline, for example the earthquake in Limón, Costa Rica. Nor is there a model that could help to establish adequate building regulations, although significant efforts are being made in Mexico to identify seismic micro-zones, particularly in the metropolitan area around Mexico City.

The threats posed by volcanoes are better understood, as more is known about the dynamics of eruptions of the most dangerous active volcanoes. Mexico, for instance, has carried out an exhaustive study of possible scenarios in the event of the eruption of Popocatépetl (just outside Mexico City), including a rigorous mapping process, warning systems, and an operational plan in the form of a signalling system. But there have been no such detailed studies of other highly dangerous volcanoes in Mexico. Throughout Central America, important work has been done with the help of CEPREDENAC (the Co-ordinating Centre for the Prevention of Natural Disasters in Central America), and several maps are now in existence. However, these do not adequately cover the risks and possible scenarios.

In the field of hydro-meteorology, the relevant authorities are generally well informed, but need to become better at predicting the progression and the trajectory of cyclones. Better research on floods is also needed, for instance in connection with the droughts associated with the El Niño phenomenon. We need a clearer understanding of this type of threat and the potential risks for agricultural production, which are particularly relevant to

campesinos and small-scale producers on rain-fed land in marginal and hillside areas.

In Mexico, various bodies are responsible for identifying the threats associated with potential risks, particularly the National Centre for the Prevention of Disasters (CENAPRED), the Department of Agriculture and Water Resources (SARH), and the Institutes of Geophysics and Geography of the Autonomous University of Mexico (UNAM), all co-ordinated through the National System for Civil Protection (SINAPROC). Costa Rica has a significant network of institutions in the various fields of earth sciences such as geology, vulcanology, and geophysics. These include the University of Costa Rica (UCR), the Costa Rican Institute of Electricity (ICE), the Seismology Observatory of Costa Rica (OVSICORI), and the National Institute of Meteorology (INM), which works in meteorology and climatology.

Guatemala and Nicaragua have reached what might be called an intermediate level in their understanding of threats and risks. Much of the relevant research takes place in place in Guatemala's National Institute of Seismology, Vulcanology, Meteorology and Hydrology (INSIVUMEH) and at Nicaragua's Institute of Earth Studies (INETER). However, their scant financial resources prevent them from retaining qualified staff and maintaining their research work. For instance, it is expected that INSIVUMEH may soon be broken up, with some areas of study being transferred to the universities, and others being privatised.

The bodies responsible for identifying threats and potential risks in El Salvador were being reorganised at the time of the study. A new Environment Ministry will have responsibility for the most important vigilance systems, and for determining regulation and control in the use of natural resources. In Honduras and Panama, the responsibility for these services lies with a range of different bodies. In both countries, the relevant institutions are experiencing serious financial difficulties, particularly the meteorological service in Honduras, where inadequate funds are undermining the stability of the workforce and jeopardising the very existence of this body.

The activities of these institutions vary greatly in quality and quantity. They consist in the production of basic and thematic maps, which show various phenomena and their respective risk zones. Projects range from those of Mexico and Costa Rica, where an Atlas of Threats is available (which in Costa Rica is integrated in a modern geographic information system), to countries like Panama, where more specific initiatives are taking place in mapping the risks of volcanoes, earthquakes, and floods. One common problem is the scale of these risk-mapping exercises. In Mexico, the 'risk atlas' is on a scale that allows for an analysis of risks but not for possible emergency scenarios to be visualised. Equally, the content of the Central American maps is general and on a very small scale, which means that they cannot be used for sensitive emergency operations.

A significant gap across the region is the lack of multi-phenomena analyses and maps. Generally, phenomena are considered independently of each other (according to the specialism of the institutions carrying out the study). This does not allow for integrated analyses of risks and the relationships between them, though this would improve the work in the field of emergency prevention in a region where all types of threat are potentially present. For the purpose of the Oxfam risk-mapping, the threats considered are those which cause the most significant damage in human, material, and economic terms: hurricanes, floods, drought, landslides, tsunamis, tidal waves, volcanic eruptions, and, particularly in Mexico and Guatemala, frosts and hailstorms.

In the case of tropical cyclones (storms and hurricanes), it is possible to identify the areas that are statistically most frequently affected. However, cyclones may also affect areas not featuring in the statistics, for example, Hurricanes Joan in 1988, Gilbert in 1993, and César in 1996. It is difficult to show the precise areas at risk of flooding and landslides in a study at this level, though significant steps have been taken (see Maps 2 and 3). Depending on the topography, coastline, and vegetation, floods and landslides are most likely to occur in the areas statistically most affected by cyclones and seismic phenomena. In general, the Atlantic Coast is more susceptible to tropical storms and floods, while the Pacific Coast is more susceptible to earthquakes, volcanic eruptions, and droughts. However, cyclones affect both of Mexico's coastlines.

The frequency of these threats varies greatly. Cyclones and storms, floods, landslides and drought occur every two to seven years. Tsunamis, earthquakes, and volcanic eruptions occur every 15 to 60 years, with some exceptions, such as the Cerro Negro volcano in Nicaragua and the Santa María (Santiaguito) volcano in Guatemala. Though the risk of volcanic eruptions and earthquakes is often deemed secondary, in that the probability of their occurrence is small, the consequences of any such catastrophe are extremely serious: the 1972 earthquake in Managua left 20,000 people dead; the 1976 Guatemala earthquake claimed 26,000 lives; the 1985 earthquake in Mexico killed between 10,000 and 20,000 people; and that in El Salvador in 1986 left 1,500 dead.

A typology of natural threats

Hurricanes

The hurricanes that affect the region originate in four principal zones: the Gulf of Tehuantepec, the Bay of Campeche, the Caribbean, and the Atlantic Region. They tend to follow trajectories which are more or less well defined, though sometimes erratic, and may or may not hit dry land (see Map 1). In Mexico, the areas most frequently affected by hurricanes are on the Pacific Coast. Hurricanes originating from near the Intertropical Convergence Zone (which is close to Central America) will progress northwards and affect the Mexican coastal areas. The hurricane season runs from June to November, with most storms occurring in September and October.

In Mexico, the probability of being directly affected by hurricanes is high, while in Central America it is relatively low, though the indirect effects are frequently experienced. The most exposed areas of Mexico experience more than five hurricanes per decade. In the worst-affected areas of Central America — the Atlantic coastline of Honduras and Nicaragua — the corresponding figure is between three and four, while the values for Panama, Costa Rica, and El Salvador are less than one.

Rapid urbanisation increases the potential for damage caused by tropical cyclones. Four of the northern states of Mexico are likely to be struck by hurricanes every two to four years, threatening some four million people in 31 coastal towns. A further two million people in another five states are exposed to the effects of

14

cyclones striking every five to seven years in another five states, and another four million people in 176 towns are vulnerable across states where hurricanes occur every eight to 26 years.

In Central America, Nicaragua and Honduras can expect 36 hurricanes or storms per century. In Nicaragua 's Atlantic Coast, the corresponding number ranges from 6 in Bluefields to 36 in Cabo Gracias a Dios, with approximately half a million people at direct risk and a further 1.3 million people exposed to indirect risk. The situation is similar in Honduras, where three-quarters of the country is affected by hurricanes, with the northern coastline most directly exposed, placing some 2.9 million people at risk. Guatemala also experiences the indirect effects of tropical cyclones, especially those originating in the western Caribbean and the Bay of Campeche, to which some two million people are exposed. In densely populated El Salvador, and also in Costa Rica and Panama, the cyclones have other characteristics and are associated with high rainfall and flooding.

Seismic activity

The region is in one of the zones of greatest seismic activity in the world, as five tectonic plates interact within it: the Cocos, Pacific, North American, Caribbean, and Nazca. Between the Pacific and North American plates a lateral slippage is occurring; between North America and Cocos, one plate is being forced under the other (a phenomenon known as 'subduction'). In both cases, significant tremors are caused which affect the region's Pacific coast.

Inland, the region is affected by continental, regional, and local fault lines. Among the most important are the San Andréas Fault in Mexico, which marks the border between the Pacific and North American plates; the Mesoamerican Trench, which divides the North American and Cocos plates (Mexico), and the Motagua-Polochic Fault (Mexico, Guatemala, and Honduras), which marks the movement of the Caribbean and North American plates (see Map 1).

Mexico experiences major earthquakes every 32 to 56 years, affecting 11 states and part of 14 more. The central and southern areas are most likely to experience earthquakes of a magnitude above 7.0 on the Richter scale, exposing some 60 million people to the phenomenon nationwide. In addition, the characteristics of the subsoil of Mexico City (where some 22 million people live) cause an approximately 400-fold amplification in seismic waves, vastly increasing the risk there.

Central America has experienced several large-scale earthquakes, some of which have occurred in the last 20 years, because the region forms a geological bridge between the Americas and is rising as a consequence of the subduction of the Cocos plate under the Caribbean plate. It is this interaction of plates which is responsible for the complexity of the geographical phenomena causing such intense seismic activity, especially on the Pacific coast (though, as noted earlier, the Atlantic coast has not been properly studied). Major seismic activity in the region occurs every 6–40 years, and secondary activity occurs more frequently. In Guatemala the four significant seismic zones cross a significant part of the surface area of the country and are associated with the interaction of plates and internal geological faults. There is a probability of earthquakes with a magnitude of 8.0 on the Richter scale occurring every 30 years, and a probability of earthquakes of 5.5–7.5 occurring every 1–15 years. Almost all of the departments of Guatemala are thus exposed to the threat of earthquakes, although they face varying levels of risk. The areas most likely to be affected are the Central Highlands (including the capital city) and the south coast, exposing approximately 6.5 million people to risk. The area of second greatest risk is in the north-eastern region and part of the north-west.

Although the pattern of seismic activity is fairly similar across the region, Honduras has reported no related disasters, despite being affected by the volcanically active areas of its neighbours and despite the influence of major fault lines in the country. This is doubtless why the subject has been studied so little in this country. However, Honduras is not out of danger: at least 80 tremors have been recorded in different parts of the country. Obviously, seismic activity in Honduras does not have the same implications as it does elsewhere, since the threats do not translate into significant risks.

The opposite is the case in El Salvador, where strong seismic activity is caused by three significant seismogenetic sources: the Motagua system of faults, the subduction of the Cocos plate, and the local system of faults. The last of these is highly dangerous, since it affects areas where there are many weaknesses (non-compacted soil), occasioning frequent cracks in rock faults that cause continuous seismic activity right across the middle of the country. A chain of young and active volcanoes is connected by a system of faults, making it even more dangerous, and affecting large areas of the country, including the metropolitan area around San Salvador. Seismic activity affects practically the whole of El Salvador, with some four million people exposed, and occurs relatively frequently, with major earthquakes taking place at intervals of between six and 20 years. Less significant tremors (<5 on the Richter scale) occur practically every year, as they do in Guatemala.

Significant seismic activity also occurs in Nicaragua. The frequency and magnitude of earthquakes here is similar to those of Guatemala and El Salvador, with seismic activity principally affecting the Pacific region, where almost one-third of the population (1.4 million people) is concentrated. The country is divided into four seismic zones, of which the most important runs from the Pacific Coast to the central volcanic chain, where there is a high risk of quakes measuring 7.0 on the Richter scale. This area includes important cities such as León, Chinandega, Managua, Masaya, and Rivas.

Since Costa Rica shares the same sources of earthquakes as the rest of Central America, the frequency and magnitude of earthquakes are similar. A complex mapping of seismic activity exists, showing three major seismic zones with approximately 1.9 million people exposed. The zone bordering the Pacific coast feels the direct impact of the Cocos and Caribbean plates. Seismic activity can reach up to 7.0 on the Richter scale, but occurs relatively deeply (deeper than 20km) and with epicentres at a short distance from major centres of population. It is worth noting that there is a 'zone of silence' in the Peninsula de Nicaya, where scientists are expecting a significant earthquake with catastrophic effects. The second zone, which includes the Central Region (interior of the country, valleys and highlands), has a moderate to low level of activity (<7) with near-surface earthquake centres (less than 20km deep). However, the potential effects are serious, since the area has the greatest concentration of the population. The third seismic zone, in the north, experiences weaker and less frequent seismic activity than the rest of the country.

Volcanic activity

Volcanic activity is highly significant, since the great volcanoes and their monogenetic fields are near to large population centres or areas of major economic activity. Though volcanic eruptions do not usually cause large-scale loss of life, and in this region are infrequent (every six to 60 years), they can cause extensive damage.

In Mexico, the volcanic strip extends from coast to coast around the 19°N parallel, with a population estimated by the Secretaría de Gobernación at about 36 million inhabitants living in the zone of influence, in 610 towns. The volcanic chain extends from the south of Mexico to the Turrialba volcano in Costa Rica, and then towards the west of Panama. CEPREDENAC has identified 582 volcanoes in the Central American region, with a total of 80 active ones, of which 25 are in Guatemala, 20 in El Salvador, 22 in Nicaragua, 11 in Costa Rica, and the rest in Panama and Honduras. (While Honduras is not thought to be at risk, CEPREDENAC registers deep cores of potential volcanoes ['focuses'] there.)

In Guatemala, the volcanoes are located on a high plateau rising to more than 4,000 metres, while in Nicaragua and El Salvador they jut out from a plain which slopes gently from the Pacific Coast. Of Guatemala's 37 volcanoes, seven are more than 3,500 metres high. The Volcán de Fuego, 45km from the capital, has been the most active and dangerous volcano since the time of the Spanish Conquest. The other active and dangerous Guatemalan volcanoes of Santa María, Santiaguito, and Pacaya threaten some 1.5 million people.

In El Salvador, volcanic and seismic activity are closely related. The volcanoes presenting the greatest threat are located in the west (Santa Ana, Izalco, San Marcelino), the central region (San Salvador, Caldera Ilopango, and San Vincente), and the east (San Miguel, Alegría or Tecapa, and Conchagua). An estimated population of about 3.9 million inhabitants is exposed, with one-third of these directly threatened by the San Salvador volcano, the most dangerous in the country.

In Nicaragua, the picture is very similar. Volcanic activity threatens 60 per cent of the population along the Pacific (where most Nicaraguans live), an estimated 1.4 million people. Important volcanoes include Cosigüina (near the Gulf of Fonseca), San Cristóbal (Chinandega), Cerro Negro, which is currently in a particularly active phase, and Momotombo (both in León), Mombacho (Granada), and Concepción (Ometepe). However, 16 more volcanoes in the same chain may begin significant activity at any moment.

Costa Rica has more than 200 volcanic focuses, of which six have shown some activity, exposing an estimated population of 690,000 inhabitants. Irazú volcano has erupted several times recently, and is very near to the city of Cartago.

16

Floods

Floods are frequent and occur almost every year to varying degrees, depending on their cause and the characteristics of each country. While floods occur inland and on both coasts, they are generally more frequent and more severe on the Atlantic Coast (though in Mexico, both coasts are hugely affected). Flooding generally occurs during the hurricane season. However, in Central America flooding occurs every couple of years, in association with the Intertropical Convergence Zone (ITCZ), especially when its effects are combined with the Odes of the East (*Las Odas del Este*). Problems associated with flooding are becoming more frequent, as more and more settlements are precariously established in high-risk zones: flood prevention through better land-use has not taken place. Soil erosion caused by deforestation and bad management of river basins has also contributed to flooding.

The many dams in the region also pose the threat of flooding, with the greatest problems occurring in Mexico and in El Salvador. Mexico has 3,211 dams in total, with 800 identified as risks (Secretaría de Gobernación 1994). In El Salvador, three important dams affect the flooding of the middle and lower parts of the River Lempa basin (Romano 1996) and have resulted in the displacement of many people and the deterioration of natural resources and the local environment.

Mexico has 47 important rivers, and SARH calculates that 70 incidences of flooding occur annually, with a potential risk to 18 million inhabitants. In three states alone (Veracruz, Sonora, and Jalisco) between 200 and 400 floods have been recorded in a 39-year period (see Map 2).

In Central America, flooding occurs in the context of complex systems of river basins which are in a state of extreme deterioration. The effects of floods are therefore devastating. In Guatemala, for example, there have been serious floods, affecting an estimated area of 23,000 km² and exposing a population of approximately 1.6 million inhabitants. The worst-affected areas are on the south coast and in the northern and north-east regions. Other areas are threatened to a lesser degree.

Honduras is particularly susceptible, because floods are associated not only with cyclones that affect large areas, but also with intense rainfall over relatively short periods. COPECO estimates that the population affected exceeds 1.4 million, mainly along the northern coastline and in the south. Floods also occur in micro-zones in marginalised areas around the cities, practically every year. This happens in the capital and in the northern industrial centres (San Pedro Sula, El Progreso, Choloma).

In El Salvador, most floods occur when the River Lempa and its tributaries in the interior of the country burst their banks. This occurs every year, especially in the lower part of the river basin, affecting an area of some 6,000 km², with a population in the order of 1.2 million. Flooding occurs as much in the urban areas, particularly in the periphery of San Salvador, as in the countryside.

Flooding occurs along both of Nicaragua's coastlines. On the Atlantic virtually all of the country's most important rivers (the Coco, the Prinzapolka, the Wawa, and the Rio Grande) flow into the sea and are easily swollen by heavy and prolonged rains. On the Pacific, the rivers are shorter and shallower and are less exposed to rain-generating phenomena, with the exception of the south-westerly winds, which bring rain because of the ITCZ. Thus floods occur every one to three years on the Atlantic Coast, and every ten years on the Pacific Coast (though the capital, Managua, floods more frequently), with some half a million people exposed. The whole length of the Atlantic Coast is affected by flooding, with important towns and many communities spread over a wide area severely affected. Since there are only about 7.5 inhabitants/km², the population at risk is in the region of about 300,000.

Flooding in Costa Rica occurs at intervals of between one and five years on both sides of the country and in the interior, with some 500,000 inhabitants threatened, in an area estimated at 5000 km², including the capital city.

Landslides

Landslides occur on slopes that have characteristics such as strong reliefs, low-resistance rocks and/or soil, and unstable structures. External factors such as seismic and volcanic activity and rainfall play a part, as do deforestation and the level of ground-water. Often landslides pass unnoticed, because they are generally associated with other larger-scale events like hurricanes, floods, and earthquakes. However, they cause great damage and many deaths in the region.

Certain zones are particularly threatened, though the records are not detailed enough to

17

show all of these throughout the rural areas. However, in urban areas the phenomenon attracts the attention of the authorities and the local population, and records are kept. The frequency with which landslides occur corresponds exactly to that of seismic and volcanic activity, floods, and strong rains.

All of the most important population centres in the region are threatened by landslides, since they are all surrounded by marginalised settlements in precarious conditions. Three critical places are Guatemala City, San Salvador, and Tegucigalpa; and, to a lesser extent, Managua and San José. Landslides associated with volcanic activity also occur in Guatemala, El Salvador, and Nicaragua, and are accompanied by lava flows, pyroclastic flows, and *lahars* (flowing masses of mingled volcanic debris and water).

Tsunamis

Tsunamis are single, giant waves caused by underwater volcanic activity or large land-slides on the seabed, although most are the result of large-scale seismic activity with epicentres on the seabed. The tidal wave that results can cause disasters many kilometres from the coast, especially when the affected regions are flat. Tsunamis have been reported in Mexico, El Salvador, and Nicaragua, although the whole of the Pacific coast is exposed to the threat.

There have been reports of this phenomenon on the Pacific coast of Mexico since 1732. Over this period, of 39 recorded tsunamis, 27 originated locally. Of the remaining 12, three came from the Aleutians, three from Japan, two from Chile, one from Alaska, one from New Zealand, one from Peru, and one from Hawaii. The 27 tsunamis that originated locally were caused by tectonic tremors, of which 94 per cent occurred on the Pacific coast and the rest hit the Gulf of Mexico. The area most affected has been Acapulco in Guerrero, where there have been 16 tsunamis, with waves measuring up to 9.5 metres. There are currently two highly threatened zones: the first extends from Baja California in the far north to Michoacán (very high risk, with 3.5 million people exposed), and the second from Guerrero to the south of the country (secondary risk, with 1.3 million people exposed).

Few tsunamis have been recorded in Central America. One occurred in El Salvador in 1902, and in September 1992 one hit the Pacific coast of Nicaragua, affecting 250km of the coastline with waves measuring 5.0m, entering inland up to 350 metres. This was caused by an earthquake measuring 7.0 on the Richter scale, with an epicentre 75km to the south-east of the coast.

Drought

Drought can affect an entire population, although its effects may be felt most directly in certain areas. While the most severe natural dangers facing the region are earthquakes, volcanoes, and hurricanes, droughts and wind erosion cause greater damage and economic losses.

Droughts now occur almost as often as floods, and it seems that in the next few years the region will go from floods to drought, or will experience both phenomena in due course. However, the data used in the mapping exercise suggest that drought occurs every two to seven years, and in some cases annually. Drought has also been associated with El Niño, a complex phenomenon now occurring on a global scale. This is currently being studied, in order that the mechanisms that activate it, as well as its evolution, can be better understood and forecast, and precautionary measures can be taken. Meanwhile, large areas of the region are suffering ever more frequently from its unpredictable impact.

In Mexico, some of the northern states are affected annually by droughts, and others every two to three years (see Map 2). It is estimated that about 27 million people may be affected, although in a study of this scale it is very difficult to determine the real impact on crops and communities.

In Central America, critical zones exist in the west of Honduras and in the north Pacific region of Nicaragua. Although other areas of Nicaragua are also affected by droughts, the incidence is less severe. A third zone is eastern El Salvador, and to a lesser degree the west of the country. Guatemala suffers drought in the northern regions and in north-east, south-east, south-west, and central areas. Lastly, Costa Rica's Chorotega and Central Pacific regions are affected. Overall in Central America, it is estimated that a total of 8.4 million people live in zones affected by drought.

Risk of threats caused by human agency

Although there is no real dividing line between risks and disasters of natural origin and those caused by human activity, these were differentiated for mapping purposes. Here, we concentrate on armed conflicts and technological emergencies, especially pollution (chemical and biological) and explosions. However, we also considered other man-made threats to the environment.

Conflicts

Central America is in transition from conflict to democracy as it undergoes a process of change after more than a decade of war and armed conflict. However, new types of conflict are now emerging, due to the social and economic injustices affecting the most impoverished and vulnerable social sectors. Guatemala and Mexico (Chiapas) merit special attention: Guatemala, because it is heading towards building a strong and lasting peace, and Mexico, because a political and military conflict is taking place against a very complex background and is having a serious impact on people's lives. Trouble-spots in the other countries could also result or already have resulted in conflicts. These conflicts may not yet be serious enough to merit emergency intervention but are worth registering, given that the development of a conflict is a process, and they could become more acute in the future. The conflicts considered here also correspond with concerns expressed by local people.

Certain aspects of these conflicts are common to the region, and are the cause of great concern: in particular, the problems associated with 'overall insecurity' because of the level of violence (among the highest in the world) and human-rights violations; economic and job insecurity against a background of inequalities; insecurity in public life (corruption, ineffective institutions); political insecurity (distrust of traditional political parties); and environmental insecurity in all its expressions. For example, in Honduras there have been serious tensions in the judicial system. More than 60 per cent of those detained in custody have not been sentenced and remain for long periods in over-crowded prisons in which riots break out at least six times a year. The land crisis of El Salvador, and the unfinished Programme of Land Reform (Programa de Transferencia de Tierra — PTT) is of great importance because it concerns the agenda left pending after the peace accords. Its non-resolution compromises any National Development Strategy (Alberto Enríquez 1997). The Washington Office on Latin America (WOLA), which is monitoring the agrarian policies of the World Bank in El Salvador, argues that land policies are critical to peace. However, the strategy proposed by the World Bank (liberalisation of the land market) and adopted by the government has left farmers and campesinos with many doubts. These previously conflicting groups now agree on the need for an agrarian policy and relief for both agrarian and bank debts.

Agrarian conflict and the struggle for access to and the defence of natural resources in Honduras are also dangerous factors. Conflicting interpretations of the Agricultural Modernisation Law (Ley de Modernización Agrícola) and the lack of a clear government policy on the administration and management of natural resources are combining to create problems. Trouble-spots are in Sico-Paulaya, which borders farmland declared an area of agrarian reform by the government, where various groups are in conflict, and Ojo de Agua, on the northern coast (lands belonging to the Garífuna people), and areas throughout the west and east of the country, and on the island of Roatán. In some of the western departments, the conflict centres on the defence of woodland, where communities are fighting influential groups who are violating the 30-year moratorium on tree-felling, agreed with the government. The situation of the chortis indians, who are fighting fiercely for their land to be restored, led to a violent protest in August 1997. This demonstration was suppressed, indicating that the crisis is now becoming significant and could spread across the country.

Forced economic migration has long affected Mexico, El Salvador, and Nicaragua. It is particularly relevant to El Salvador, because one-fifth (1.5 million) of Salvadorans living abroad are in the USA, many of them at serious risk of deportation. Through monthly remittances, these people make a significant contribution to the country's economy: some US$1,086 million, which represents nearly 10 per cent of the Gross National Product, far more than that received in aid from the USA (see Table 1).

Table 1: Remittances from Salvadorans in USA and aid from USA (in millions of US dollars)

Year	Monthly payments to families	US aid
1991	518.0	219.6
1992	686.0	294.6
1993	884.0	220.3
1994	958.0	76.4
1995	1,000.0	38.9
1996	1,086.0	41.8
Total	**5,132.0**	**936.2**

Until 1995 deportations averaged 1,800 a year, but the trend is ever increasing. Salvadoran nationals represented about 3.5 per cent of those deported from the USA before a new immigration law came into force on 1 April 1997.

The *maquilas* (assembly plants) and pressure on local resources are important issues in Honduras and El Salvador. For instance, in Choloma (Honduras), the total number of industries (around 50) is expanding, but this growth does not feature in any municipal development plan to cater for the demand for services from the large number of people seeking work there. An estimated 70,000 workers are currently living in very difficult conditions in which very few of their basic needs are being met. Choloma and the surrounding areas do not have the necessary absorption capacity, and the present situation is likely to create a trouble-spot: in addition to being a significant site of industrial conflict, the area is rife with violence and delinquency, and there is a proliferation of sexually transmitted diseases.

In the industrial belt in the north of Honduras, San Pedro Sula shows an especially high incidence of HIV/AIDS for Central America; 57 per cent of the recorded cases in the region are in Honduras, and are concentrated in San Pedro Sula. Given the behaviour of the syndrome and the speed with which it advances, it could soon have a significant impact on the nation's health. It has been predicted that life expectancy at birth could be reduced by up to 30 per cent by the year 2000. It is currently estimated that 80,000 people are carriers of the virus, two-thirds of whom are male. Most are in the 15–34 year-old age group (72 per cent), of whom 65 per cent live in San Pedro Sula or around the capital city.

Technology-related emergencies

A technology-related emergency involves spillages, leaks, fire, or the explosion of any toxic or dangerous substance, object, or product. The threat is present in all the countries, particularly in Mexico, where on average 775 fires and explosions are recorded annually, mainly in and around Mexico City, Nuevo León, Sonora, Baja California, Chihuahua, and Guanajuato (Secretaría de Gobernación 1994).

In Central America, the greatest threats are from the operations of oil companies and the transportation of toxic substances. For example, 80 per cent of the oil pipeline crossing Costa Rica from the north-east to the south-west is above ground, and at Cartago there is a battery of storage tanks above ground level without any system of safety control. In Managua, the refinery has leaked phenol into the groundwater that is the source of 30 per cent of the capital's water supply. The same is happening in Honduras, where a pipeline is threatening the city of Tela. Meanwhile, according to the Honduran Red Cross, combustible material is transported without safety regulations by road (there is no national railway network in Honduras) from the principal ports to various destinations inland.

With the closure of Penwalt in Nicaragua, Central America is supplied with liquid chlorine from Mexico, which is transported through Guatemala along the Panamerican Highway, without any safety controls. None of the Central American countries has any expertise in dealing with this substance in the event of an emergency.

Another risk worthy of mention is the high probability of fires in three of the hospitals in Honduras, where the electricity systems are very old and overloaded: it would be impossible to evacuate patients in the event of a fire, as the emergency exits were sealed in the 1980s, so that political prisoners undergoing treatment could not escape.

Abuses of natural resources

The entire region is in the midst of a major environmental crisis, which has contributed substantially to the increase in dangerous situations, some of which would, in combination with natural occurrences, result in disasters. The threats vary in magnitude, although several of them are serious in all the countries. The mapping exercise picked out those that could trigger irreversible processes with serious consequences for the future of the region.

The most sensitive of these threats is deforestation. In Mexico the destruction of forests is most advanced in the south, especially in Chiapas, where the situation has been aggravated by armed conflict. It is still not possible to quantify the impact of the militarisation of the area (for example the increased consumption of firewood to meet the needs of military personnel, and deforestation for the establishment of mobile bases and for land/air operations). In reality, the process of deforestation in Mexico has accelerated throughout the whole country. It is calculated that 260,000km^2 of land are now in a state of advanced desertification, principally in the central areas. This is resulting in the loss of fertile soil, which is calculated at 2.8 tonnes per hectare per year, affecting agricultural production and, because of widespread sedimentation, the efficiency of dams for the generation of energy.

In Central America, El Salvador and Costa Rica are the most seriously affected countries, followed by Guatemala, Nicaragua, and Honduras. In El Salvador, only 12 per cent of the land area is under forest cover, including just 2 per cent covered by primary woodland. It was estimated by the Ministry of Planning in 1993 that the annual loss of fertile soil in El Salvador was 500 tonnes per hectare per year, with the former conflict areas of Chalatenango, Cabañas, Cuscatlán, and Morazán the most badly affected (UNDP 1997). Costa Rica has a deforestation rate of 50,000 hectares a year, and only 25 per cent of its forest cover now remains. Its government announced in 1990 that agricultural land has now been exhausted, as the land left is not suitable for production.

In Guatemala, the problem is equally bad. The deforestation rate is estimated at 90,000 hectares a year, with a loss of 51 per cent of forest land overall, and 65 millions of tons of fertile soil nationally (CONAMA 1995), principally in the north and the Petén (a rainforest area). In Nicaragua, it is estimated that 100,000 hectares a year are affected, and in Honduras the rate is 80,000 hectares a year, particularly in the south and west. There are also indications that salinisation is occurring in southern Honduras, where salt has been detected in ground-waters.

Forest fires are on the increase, because of the frequent droughts occurring in the region. The problem is serious in Mexico and Honduras. In Mexico, fires occur in large areas of the country, while in Honduras most of the country is affected, with an annual loss of more than 30,000 hectares a year.

The loss of forest cover is contributing to diminishing water resources. Most of the drainage basins have changed their hydrological characteristics, causing great flooding in the rainy season and reduced flow in the dry season. Throughout the region, there is concern at the increasingly frequent 'deaths' of many small rivers which previously irrigated the land and were fundamental in meeting basic needs, while large rivers have seen a huge reduction in the water supply. A clear example is that of the River Lempa in El Salvador: from 1985 to 1993, its capacity for collecting water diminished from 11,260m^3 to 4,482 m^3.

Air, soil, and water pollution is another common and serious threat. The SARH calculates that 50 per cent of Mexico's drainage basins are contaminated with organic industrial waste (61 per cent) and urban waste (30 per cent), resulting in serious pollution of supplies of water for various uses, including human consumption. Mexico City alone produces 24 per cent of the country's air pollution, with two other major towns responsible for seven per cent between them.

Soil and water pollution is also significant in Central America. For instance, in addition to the serious pollution of water resources by pesticides, organic waste, and industrial waste which affects the whole of El Salvador, the entire eastern region will soon face a crisis because of water shortages: after 2000, demand will outstrip the available resources by 24 per cent, a situation which translates into an imminent risk. The country's Pacific coast is in a critical situation, as it is the only area where liquid waste and river water (both polluted) are discharged, and is suffering serious deterioration of its coastal and marine resources. The River Acelhuate, where the waste from San Salvador is deposited, becomes a tributary of the River Lempa (upstream), which therefore ends up being an agent of pollution along the whole of its course.

Agrochemicals are a significant source of soil and water pollution in the region, and have a noticeable impact on human health. In Guatemala, the areas affected are in the centre and south of the country, resulting in up to 30,000 incidences of pesticide poisoning, and serious water and soil pollution. In Nicaragua, the Ministry of Health estimates that more than 1,200 people per 100,000 inhabitants in two departments on the Pacific coast are poisoned, and there is considerable pollution of water sources (both at surface level and underground) and soil. In Costa Rica, the use of pesticides has doubled to the current figure of 12,000 tons/year, resulting in drastic pollution of rivers and coasts, especially the basins of the River Tárcoles and the River Bermúdez .

Mining operations also cause pollution, as in the case of the open-mining operations in the north of Costa Rica and in the Tilarán mountains. (These operations are causing serious conflicts with local people.) In Honduras, the mining operations around Lake Yojoa have caused extreme pollution of water and soil. In Nicaragua, there is pollution in the mining areas of the Atlantic Coast.

Pollution from rubbish merits special attention. The case of Guatemala illustrates the magnitude of the problems. The city has only one waste disposal site, 'El Trébol', which receives approximately 1,200 tons of waste a day. The rest is burnt in the open air or disposed of in 50 underground rubbish dumps around the city. Industrial waste and waste from hospitals in Guatemala City is collected along with household waste and taken to rubbish tips, without any safety controls. A similar situation occurs in Costa Rica, where 1,400 tons of waste are produced each day, and only 40 per cent is disposed of adequately. The problem is also very acute in El Salvador, especially given the high concentration of the population in urban areas.

Evaluation and levels of risks

Once threats have materialised, they become risks, the magnitude of which varies according to various factors. Our assessment of exposure to threats therefore focused on demographic distribution, economic infrastructure and activity, general infrastructure and services, and whether safety regulations exist and are observed.

The general characteristics of the areas classified as high-risk zones are as follows.

- They face various physical risks (earthquakes, volcanic activity, floods, landslides and avalanches, drought, tidal waves, hurricanes, pollution, fires, and explosions).
- They are exposed to combinations of threats, which generally result in a chain-reaction of risks.
- They tend to be areas with a high level of economic production, with infrastructure and basic services, making them zones of strategic economic importance for the region and for the countries in question.
- The communication systems and the road network are generally good.
- There is a high population density (almost 60 per cent of the regional population is concentrated there).

A country-by-country summary (Table 2) describes the most important risks faced, according to the criteria indicated above.

Table 2: Areas of priority for emergency work

Country	Regions	Level of risk
Mexico	Central and South (15-32 states)	Very high
	North and border	High to moderate
Guatemala	Metropolitan	Very high
	Central	Very high
	South-west	Very high
	North	High
	North-west	High to moderate
	North-east, Petén	
Honduras	North-west	Very high
	West	Very high
	South	Very high
	Central	High to moderate
	North-east	Moderate
El Salvador	Central-south	Very high
	Eastern-south	Very high
	East-south	High to moderate
	Rest of the country	High to moderate
Nicaragua	Pacific	Very high
	Central and Atlantic	High to moderate
Costa Rica	Central	Very high
	Chorotega	High
	Huetar Atlántico	High to moderate

Mexico

Mexico is a country with an area of about 2 million km² and and a population of 82 million inhabitants. The key factors in the many disasters it has suffered may be political, economic, or social. All too often, the people most exposed to danger are ignorant of the potential risk in which they live. Despite the great diversity of factors that come into play, two variables are constant: poverty and unplanned human settlements.

The mapping exercise focused particularly on the Popocatépetl volcano ('Popo'), in the centre of the country, and the conflicts in the south (Chiapas). The former will be covered here, while the latter will be covered later in the study. The case of Popocatépetl illustrates just one of many possible scenarios faced by Mexico.

Popocatépetl is Mexico's second-highest peak (5,452m), lying 55km south-east of Mexico City and 45km from the city of Puebla. In spite of the potential danger facing these important population centres, including one of the biggest cities in the world, Popo has hardly been studied from a geological point of view. Recently, there have been significant studies of the history of its eruptions and the way it functions, to determine possible scenarios that might occur in the event of a huge eruption. Popo has a very complex eruptive history, but only the most recent 23,000-year period is known about in great detail. The principal dangers associated with Popo are the following.

- **Lava flow and domes of lava:** a flow of molten and white-hot material that follows the morphology of the land. The flow advances slowly and rarely presents a danger to human life, but buries and burns everything that comes into its path. The volcano has a Tholoid dome, which was formed in March 1996 inside the crater. This has not grown much (only 20 per cent of the volume of the crater), and so has not reached the rim of the crater and does not represent a danger, according to a UNAM study. The outer limits of the danger area are Amecameca, San Andrés, Atlixco, and Tetela del Volcán.

- **Viscous pyroclastic flows:** explosive eruptions which produce materials composed of toxic gases and fragments of rock, pumice, and debris. These flows travel at great speed down the sides of the volcano, destroying and burning everything in their path. In the past, the volcano has registered this type of activity.

Some of the communities threatened by this phenomenon are Ozumba, Amecameca, Tochimilco, and Atlixco.

- **Lahars (mudslides and related phenomena):** a mixture of water and fragments of rock, capable of dragging large objects across great distances, lahars tend to flow through gullies, as the affected areas are found in zones of low relief, but they travel farther than any other volcanic flow. The most exposed places are Cuautla, Yecapixtla, Izúcar de Matamoros, and many others around the volcano.

- **Huge rockfalls (avalanches of debris):** the collapse of part of the volcano, due to the magma being forced up from below, or to intense seismic activity, can cause flows of materials which travel at great speed (100m/second) and are capable of carrying entire parts of the volcano across hundreds of metres. There is now a possibility that part of Popo's actual cone will collapse, particularly towards the southern side, which could provoke a vast avalanche of debris.

- **Various materials in free fall (ashes, pyroclastic material, ballistic projectiles):** these materials are emitted during explosive eruptions, either ballistically or vertically into the atmosphere to form a column of volcanic material which can reach several kilometres in height. In this case, the wind determines where particles are deposited. When this material accumulates, it can cause roofs to collapse and it contaminates vegetation and springs. Popo has registered several eruptions of this kind. Ash can reach the size of gravel in the immediate environs, while farther away the fall of ash causes health problems, as well as damaging crops and blocking drainage systems.

- **Volcanic gases:** during fumarolic activity (when hot gases and vapours issue from holes in the volcano) and actual eruptions, the gassy component of the magma is made up of water vapour and, in smaller proportions, a wide variety of gases with very toxic components. Breathing in these gases causes vomiting, asphyxia, and cardiovascular stress. They cause harm to crops, contaminate water, and corrode metal structures.

The volcano and its areas of influence have been divided into three wide rings (with the crater at the centre); within each of them, the levels of risks are estimated as follows: 100,000 people at very high risk, 300,000 people at high risk, and one million people at moderate risk (Dirección General de Protección Civil, Secretaría de Gobernación 1997). However, civil-society organisations (CSOs) estimate that the numbers threatened are more like two million.

There is little information about the economic activities of the communities and states concerned, though CENAPRED is estimating the damage that an eruption would cause in the event of various probable scenarios. Access roads to the volcano are relatively good in the State of Mexico. However, many stretches are at high risk of being buried by volcanic materials, as they are intersected by great gullies, through which volcanic material would run. Housing infrastructure and public services are also exposed, as is the economy, given that 70 per cent of production is agricultural. In reality, it would be difficult for the communities at risk to withstand the magnitude of the threat. In fact, the town of Amecameca is built on the earlier settlement of Ameca, which was buried in a previous eruption.

The situation of Popo is not an isolated case in Mexico, but is part of a complex system of threats facing the country, especially in the high-risk zones. For instance, a similar situation can be seen in the case of the Chichonal volcano in Chiapas and the disaster that befell the *Zoque* indians, who now face the greatest challenge in their history: the survival of their ethnic group following the eruption of this volcano in April 1982.

Central America

The people of Central America face a situation that is no less bleak. The levels of risks exposed in the mapping exercise can be illustrated by three factors: the recurrence of events with serious implications for the development of the region, a concrete example of which is provided by Guatemala; the damage caused to the population, the infrastructure, and the economy (which can be seen in El Salvador); and the potential risk, as seen in the case of Costa Rica. Using these examples we can examine three basic aspects in the evaluation of risks: What has happened? What are the implications of present threats? And what can we expect in the future?

Throughout history, Central America, with a total population of about 30 million, has experienced disasters. In the Zones of Risk

(see Table 2), recent major events have included the earthquakes in Managua (1972), Guatemala (1976), San Salvador (1986), and Costa Rica (1991), and Hurricanes Fifi in Honduras (1974) and Joan in Nicaragua (1988) [and Mitch in 1998 – Ed.]. These are extreme events in a geographic region where many communities are annually subjected to physical and social displacement as a result of smaller-scale disasters.

Guatemala

The capital city of Guatemala has been moved twice after being destroyed by disasters. The settlement in the valley of Almolonga (now Ciudad Vieja) was razed in September 1541 by an avalanche from the Agua volcano. The city of Santiago founded afterwards in the valley of Pancoy (now Antigua Guatemala) was finally abandoned in 1775, after suffering constant calamities as a result of volcanic eruptions and strong earthquakes, culminating in the earthquake of Santa Marta in 1773. Today's Guatemala City lies about 45km away from the Antigua, in a location even more exposed to seismic threats. Catastrophic earthquakes occurred there in 1917, 1918, and 1976.

Other important population centres in the priority zones have also been affected by disastrous events. For example, the 'great earthquake of the West' in 1902 measured 8.2 on the Richter scale and caused serious damage in all the towns in the highlands, leaving at least 2,000 people dead. Months later, the Santa María volcano ejected eight cubic kilometres of sand and ash in 36 hours, which covered almost ten towns and the provincial capitals of Quetzaltenango and San Marcos, causing the deaths of at least 1,000 people and serious damage to agriculture. Twenty-nine years later, a second crater, called Santiaguito, opened up and has been active to this day. A combination of the volcanic activity of Santiaguito and heavy rains laid waste to the town of El Palmar, testifying to the destructive potential of the River Samalá (stirred up by the quantity of sand and volcanic ash) along the length of its course to its mouth on the Pacific coast. Important population centres along this track could share a similar fate.

Apart from these momentous catastrophes, there have been other events caused by torrential rains that have flooded the zone identified in the mapping. Hurricanes, droughts, landslides, and other devastating threats have similarly affected the area. For

24

example, the mapping exercise identified various rivers which cause great flooding along their courses in the south. According to local people, near its mouth the river reaches such a high level that parents hang their children in hammocks from the tallest tree-tops to prevent the turbulent waters from reaching them.

The study's examination of past and probable events in high-risk zones confirms the impression, immortalised in the local saying, that 'no corner of Guatemala is safe'.

El Salvador

El Salvador is significantly affected by flooding and droughts in the high-risk zones. In the last 50 years, more than 25 serious floods have been registered. CEPRODE's assessments of the damage caused in this period indicate that more than 26,000 families have been seriously affected by floods, more than 6,000 houses damaged, 43,000 people injured, and 17,000 hectares of crops destroyed. On 16 October 1993, strong tides in Sonsonate and La Libertad resulted in the water entering a considerable distance inland, which caused serious flooding in the communities living in the coastal zone.

Severe droughts have also occurred, particularly in the east, with serious repercussions for agriculture. The Ministry of the Environment recorded losses of more than 6,000 tons of basic grains in 1992. The 1991 drought caused losses of more than US$37m in the production of basic grains, and a reduction in coffee production of 35–50 per cent. The drought also had serious implications for the energy industry, as there was drastic rationing, which caused daily losses in the order of US$125,000, apart from the domestic losses not quantified.

Seismic and volcanic activity also has serious repercussions:

- The earthquake of 3 May 1965 shook the areas surrounding San Salvador, leaving 10,000 families homeless.

- The 19 June 1982 earthquake was felt almost right across the country, and was also perceptible in Guatemala, Honduras, Nicaragua, and Costa Rica. It caused great material damage: 1,630 houses were destroyed, and 5,000 families left homeless.

- In 1982 a colossal earthquake occurred near the top of the San Salvador volcano, affecting various areas to the north-east of San Salvador. The cause was attributed to large masses of soil becoming loose, due to the

intensive rains and the extensive deforestation of the volcano. These factors, together with the poor planning of human settlements, created favourable conditions for the disaster, which left 500 dead and 2,400 injured, and destroyed 120 houses (CEPRODE estimates). The losses in terms of housing were calculated by the Ministry of Planning in 1993 at US$418,765, and 20 hectares of crops were lost. There were also health problems, job losses, reductions in family incomes, and an increase in public spending for the purpose of reconstruction.

- On 10 October 1986, one of the biggest earthquakes ever recorded affected the whole of the population of San Salvador, leaving 1,500 dead, 45,600 houses destroyed, economic losses in the region of US$1,500m, 250,000 families homeless, and 415 public buildings damaged (according to the Ministry of Planning).

The risks associated with volcanic activity are high, because the population is concentrated around the most important volcanoes in the country. According to CEPRODE, the population exposed reaches 3.9 million, taking into account some of the smaller volcanoes. Both CEPRODE and USAID calculate that in the last 100 years damage in the region of US$2,000m has been caused by earthquakes and volcanoes; more than 60,000 houses have been damaged, and 500,000 families have suffered injuries.

Landslides associated with seismic activity and intensive rains occur frequently in the country, blocking roads, damaging the crops of small and medium-scale producers, and affecting important urban centres. In 1995, several landslides were reported in the settlements on Lake Ilopango, a consequence of the earthquake that occurred in San Salvador.

Costa Rica

Two-thirds of the population of 3.3 million is concentrated in the central valley (designated a Very High Risk Zone in Table 2). More than half of these people live in the metropolitan area of San José and the seven provincial capitals. The country is predominantly urban, as the rest of the population is concentrated in a few medium-sized cities (between 40,000 and 85,000 people), or in small rural communities. San José is the country's commercial centre and forms the axis of the so-called Central Corridor, of which the outer limits are the ports of Limón and

Puntarena. Ninety-five per cent of the country's imports and exports are concentrated in these two cities, and certain strategically important industries are based there: the oil refineries, for example.

The country's production base is fundamentally rural, with products like coffee, bananas, sugar, cotton, and meat dominating in terms of commerce and exports. Tourism, based on the country's beaches and eco-tourist ventures, is also important in the national economy.

The population, economy, and infrastructure are therefore concentrated precisely in the zones that are at high risk of seismic activity, volcanoes, floods, hurricanes (indirect effects), and droughts. In addition, other risks, whether natural (avalanches, rockfalls, etc.) or of human agency (pollution and technology-related emergencies), can also be triggered. In the last 10 years, the Institute of Meteorology has intervened in 33 emergencies of hydro-meteorological origin alone, which have caused losses estimated in total at US$ 670 million. The effects of storms and hurricanes (principally because of floods) thus have significant consequences for the national economy.

Because of the 'zone of silence' off the coasts of Guanacaste, a huge earthquake is expected in the Chorotega region, which will shake the nation in every sense. In addition, the growth of marginal communities around the capital city has resulted in a significant risk of floods and landslides. According to the Co-ordinator of these communities, the people face annual flooding, during which drinking water and dirty water get mixed, settlements are destroyed by flood waters, houses collapse, and so on. A local risk map, drawn up for the community of Los Guidos, reveals its precarious situation and illustrates the great degree of risk experienced by more than 50 marginal communities around the capital city. In the centre of the country, volcanic activity is very frequent and, although not of great magnitude (< 6.5 on the Richter scale), earthquakes occur at surface level and are capable of great destruction.

We conclude this section with a table that summarises the levels of risk and impact that are associated with hurricanes. [Hurricane Mitch, estimated to be the third-strongest hurricane of the century in Central America, struck the region in November 1998, after this report was written, and therefore too late to be considered in detail. – Ed.]

Table 3: Hurricanes and damage caused across the region

Country/Occurrence	Human cost	Economic effects	Losses (in US$ millions)
Honduras, 1974 Hurricane Fifi	8,000 dead 600,000 affected	GNP: -4.3% Agriculture: -8%	US$ 540
Nicaragua, 1988 Hurricane Joan	120 dead 300,000 affected	GNP: -2% Agriculture: -10%	US$ 839
Costa Rica, 1996 Hurricane César	39 dead 500,000 affected	GNP: -0.7% Agriculture: -1%	US$ 151
Nicaragua 1996 Hurricane César	9 dead 110,000 affected	GNP: -0.3% Agriculture: -0.2%	US$ 50.5

3 Assessment of vulnerability

Natural disasters, we assume, detonate crises in contexts of social, economic, environmental, and political instability, bringing to light a series of hidden conflicts and potentially dangerous situations. Here we seek to identify the most crucial problems of groups living in high-risk zones that make them vulnerable to, and in the end victims of, disasters.

Technical focus on vulnerability

Vulnerability is defined in technical terms as the proportion of human lives, assets, and economic activity that could be affected in a given place should a given disaster occur. This allows us to evaluate the potential damage and thus to construct scales of risks, in view of the probability of a destructive phenomenon occurring. In addition, it allows us to calculate the potential damage and its costs, and compare them with the cost of preventive actions to minimise the damage. We can therefore provide the people who make political decisions with the tools to make those decisions and also persuade them of what needs to be taken into account when formulating disaster-prevention policies.

These objectives have not yet been achieved in Mexico and Central America, and research is still in its infancy. Previous studies tended to focus on destructive natural phenomena rather than on vulnerability. Costa Rica is a case in point. There are plenty of data available in the Geographic Information System (GIS) of the National Emergencies Commission (CNE), but they consist of information which is relevant essentially to the physical aspects of disasters, rather than their economic and social effects, although Costa Rica is one of the countries where the investigation of natural risks is most advanced. In Guatemala, CONRED (the National Commission for the Reduction of Disasters) intends to carry out another important study, but there are no firm plans. This situation can be explained principally by the insufficiency of data; lack of inter-institutional co-ordination; difficulties in obtaining existing data; incompatible data; and the frequent absence of a GIS, or inadequate use of one where it does exist. Local studies of vulnerability have rarely been based on sufficiently precise studies of phenomena. For example, there is a lack of micro-seismic studies, which makes it impossible to undertake reliable studies of levels of infrastructural vulnerability in the region, whether public or private.

It is very difficult to establish the relationship between destructive phenomena and damage caused. Sometimes the predictive and planning systems used have been based on the experiences of other countries (for example, US systems have been used to determine the effects of earthquakes and hurricanes on housing). However, these systems are rarely adapted to local conditions. For example, in the majority of cases, building regulations do not consider dead weights on the roofs of houses, thus ignoring the possibility of deposits of volcanic ash. Similarly, the force of winds considered in these regulations does not correspond to the forces normally reached by hurricanes affecting the countries in the region.

As the present levels of vulnerability cannot be established, evaluations of the potential consequences of natural disasters have tended to focus on past events. It is therefore difficult to form a reasonably long-term view to enable comparisons to be made and to establish the relevance of the impact of past events to potential events in the future.

For all these reasons, analyses of vulnerability are severely inadequate. The principal initiatives are essentially concerned with the vulnerability of strategically important buildings such as schools and hospitals, with housing being a secondary concern. In fact, hospitals were the subject of the first significant attempts to use a cost–benefit methodology to evaluate the economic consequences of damage caused by natural disasters.

- The OEA/ECHO programme for the reduction of vulnerability in the education sector represents an advance in this field, although it is only at the pilot stage (covering 1,500 schools in Central America out of a total of 4,500) and concentrates on the structure of the buildings. The results of the studies are not yet available, although some revealing information is now available: in Honduras, for instance, 55 per cent of schools are designated high-risk and highly vulnerable; and in Guatemala, more than 60 per cent of schools are designated very vulnerable, having been constructed without reference to building regulations.

• Programmes to analyse and reduce the vulnerability of hospitals have also been carried out, particularly in Costa Rica, where many hospitals were shown to be seriously vulnerable. These have all been reconstructed using special structural engineering techniques, financed at great cost by the Costa Rican authorities (Caja Costarricense de Seguro Social). According to the National Disaster Prevention Unit of the Ministry for Health and Social Security in Guatemala, of 36 hospitals, 35 per cent were designated very vulnerable. In Mexico, according to the Mexican Red Cross, of 86 hospitals, 80 per cent were designated very vulnerable.

Few studies have dealt with the technical vulnerability of buildings, especially domestic housing. One important study, carried out in 1995 by CEPREDENAC/OEA, is worth noting. It was incorporated into the Regional Plan of Human Settlements and Housing, under the auspices of Habitat II in 1996. An action plan for Central America identifies the municipalities and areas of towns most vulnerable to natural disasters, with the emphasis on the most precarious settlements.

Vulnerable housing is a critical issue in the region. Firstly, building regulations seldom address the reality of the risks, given the absence of detailed studies of zones of seismic activity. Secondly, limited financial resources mean that these regulations are not observed. And thirdly, there is major corruption in dealings between construction firms and the bodies responsible for ensuring that building regulations are observed, particularly when the buildings in question are in earthquake-prone zones. According to the information available, Honduras, Nicaragua, and Guatemala are the most vulnerable in this respect, followed by El Salvador and Mexico, and finally Costa Rica and Panama.

A good example of the above is the case of the Mexico City earthquake in 1985, which killed as many as 30,000 people and left approximately 60,000 homeless. It was clear that building regulations had not been observed, especially those prohibiting construction in areas of high seismic activity. An example of this is that 60 per cent of the buildings currently standing in Mexico City have been built in danger zones, with no explanation to date of how this happened. The result is a city with 18 million inhabitants which runs the risk of being destroyed in the next earthquake.

Political focus on vulnerability

Political vulnerability is defined as the inverse value of a community's level of autonomy in taking decisions that affect it. That is, the greater the autonomy, the less the political vulnerability of the community.

In countries with highly centralised governments, political vulnerability has two facets. Firstly, it is harder for a community to attract the attention of decision makers at a national level. Secondly, local communities find it hard to formulate their own solutions to a given problem, and to apply local knowledge and resources to their solutions, thus limiting the need for external help to that which is strictly necessary.

However, in Mexico and Central America a process of decentralisation and municipal autonomy now features prominently on the agendas of leading decision makers. Given the framework of the democratisation that is taking place in the region, the issue of autonomy has come to the forefront. However, it is a long-term process, and there are still many problems preventing greater progress. What has occurred so far has been a process of 'deconcentration' rather than decentralisation. That is, a series of problems and responsibilities have been transferred to municipalities, but without the resources to deal with the problems and to address social needs. Given the high levels of poverty which these municipalities face, they cannot be autonomous in dealing with the risks and consequences of disasters, whatever their origin.

In terms of political vulnerability, the countries of Central America are among the poorest in the world (with the exception of Costa Rica) and the most indebted. They have no economic or financial autonomy or food security, since they are very dependent on external help in tackling development problems, including dealing with disasters. The management of natural disasters is related to political systems that are in deep crisis, and are characterised by administrations which are greatly tainted by corruption, impunity, and unethical behaviour. This does not inspire the confidence of the population as a whole, nor of the aid agencies that work on disaster prevention or intervene in emergencies. For example, from 1982 to 1983 the region of Guanacaste in Costa Rica suffered a severe drought with great losses to agricultural production. The money to compensate for the losses sustained during the drought and the earthquake in San Isidro El General was administered through the National Emergency Fund of the National Emergencies Commission (CNE) and directly by the Presidential Office. In 1985 it was discovered that fraud, estimated initially to be worth US$300,000 and rising with time to almost US$3m, had occurred. In 1986 a number of people were accused, including ex-President Monge, ex-Vice President Arauz, and Monge's former Personal Assistant. In 1994, after a trial lasting 10 years, Monge and Arauz were exonerated of any blame.

This incident undermined public confidence in the CNE and was an important factor in its lack of progress and consolidation. In addition, as the scandal was at its peak, the Office of Civil Defence underwent various management changes which prevented continuity in its work, leaving disaster professionals frustrated at the slow progress. This incident illustrates how levels of vulnerability can be increased by the way in which disasters are managed, as much as by the disasters themselves.

On the other hand, in some respects disasters are being managed in a positive way. In general, all the countries are making an effort to establish rules for international aid in emergency situations, through certain procedures that must be followed through the foreign offices of each country. El Salvador and Costa Rica have made most progress in this matter. However, although these measures can help to manage external aid and channel aid from friendly countries, they can also complicate matters for international NGOs already in the area. In addition, it is difficult for organisations to channel significant quantities of resources without the security of knowing that they will reach those who need them most. Similarly, organisations cannot know for certain whether resources will reach the communities for which they are destined, and the groups they aim to reach.

In Mexico, the situation is similarly somewhat complicated, in that although the government does not ask for help once an emergency has been declared, it cannot itself help those in need. The vulnerability of communities affected by a disaster is obvious, as they do not have the capacity to manage their own problems themselves, but must rely on others to help them, through actions which may or may not be effective, owing to economic policy or party politics. The problem is aggravated when, because of political polarisation, no decision is taken, or a decision is made too late, in both cases with serious consequences for local communities. Recent such cases include the drought during which the governments of Honduras and Nicaragua refused to declare a state of emergency for political reasons. This prevented the international community from giving assistance. For example, UNDP in Nicaragua has resources available for emergencies that it does not commit, unless it receives an official request from the government and a state of emergency is declared.

One interesting aspect concerns compliance with the Code of Conduct for aid in emergencies. Many organisations consulted on the matter said that in general their governments observed the Code, though we consider this to be dubious. For instance, in Costa Rica, the First Lady has repeatedly delivered food to disaster areas, distributing it directly and with no controls, and frequently in a form and a quantity (including products not suited to the local needs) that promote dependency. But such actions do get wide press coverage, which may of course be the intention.

In other cases, politicians capitalise on emergencies to gain votes. For example, in August 1997 President Reina of Honduras visited the drought-affected departments of Valle and Choluteca and promised the communities that in the next term of government (if his party won the November elections) he would construct a dam in the area to ensure irrigation and to reduce their vulnerability. The main *campesino* organisation in Honduras, the COCOCH, says that the irrigation is destined for the large producers in the area and that *campesino* farmers will continue to be exposed to drought and increasingly difficult conditions, given the salinisation occurring in that area of the country.

Finally, and still on the theme of the Code of Conduct, the independence of NGOs in their humanitarian aid work is not respected, particularly in Mexico and Nicaragua. Nor is information exchange being facilitated in emergency situations, which makes it difficult for NGOs to act effectively, as occurred in the case of the drought in Honduras and Nicaragua.

Social focus on vulnerability

The very nature of underdevelopment means that disasters are a secondary issue in the context of the many needs that must be met.

In Mexico and Central America, understanding of disasters and their management is still limited. The incapacity of governments to solve the primary problems that characterise countries with a low level of development makes for a situation in which disaster-response is not a priority. The primary problems include the elimination of the extreme poverty suffered by broad sectors of society; economic and technological dependence on other countries; the great deficit in public finances; the need to improve and expand the infrastructure for development; the need for decent housing; and a lack of jobs. Governments seem to act on the assumption that disasters may or may not occur, and so it makes more sense to concentrate first on solving or addressing the more immediate needs which, while they have been urgent for decades, are becoming increasingly acute.

There is a tendency to focus on problems fiscally in terms of projected risks and vulnerabilities, rather than from a social perspective. Only one organisation, The Network of Social Studies for the Prevention of Natural Disasters in Latin America (LA RED), has been concerned with generating knowledge and proposals for a study of social vulnerability; it has promoted some very valuable new concepts. This has influenced organisations such as the Latin American Faculty of Social Sciences (FLACSO) (regional), CEPRODE (El Salvador), UNAM (Mexico), and the German organisation GTZ (regional), among others, to consider human factors of vulnerability in their analyses and studies. Apart from these isolated instances, there are no serious studies of social vulnerability. The problem centres on the difficulty of obtaining detailed information about local risks. As a result, there is a lack of real tools for decision making — tools which could influence decision-makers and direct their policies, and which might help to solve the underlying problems.

A regional view of social vulnerability

Although Central America experiences more disasters than almost anywhere else in the world, and these disasters have common roots in the natural, socio-economic, and political environment of the region as a whole, few studies have focused on a regional analysis or strategy. Existing studies have tended to focus on individual cases in isolation from their regional context. Almost without exception, the methodologies and techniques used to date have had a local focus, concentrating on places where the risks of disasters and emergencies have been experienced.

The uniqueness of the mapping exercise described here is that it was obliged to adopt a regional focus in order to analyse the vulnerability of the communities exposed to the risks of disasters in Mexico and Central America. It is a complex task to carry out a regional or national analysis of the vulnerability of communities in the face of disasters, in that the focus has always been on the characteristics of a past or probable event, usually with the aim of taking steps for preparedness and response. An analysis of vulnerability, however, is more useful for determining necessary steps for preparedness, mitigation, and response.

Studies of vulnerability with a local focus tend to employ detailed analyses of the following: the systems of production in an area; the infrastructure and access to services; communications and transport systems; the dominant culture and the capacities of local agents and communities for organisation and mobilisation; and the degree of preparedness of a group or community in the face of possible emergencies. At a regional level it is almost impossible to evaluate all of these, given the diversity of situations and the near impossibility of ensuring field trips and interviews across such a wide area. Thus, in order to adopt a focus and methodology which allowed risks and vulnerabilities and the factors common to each to be visualised on a regional and national scale, the study sacrificed elements of the rich diversity of different localities, except in some cases where field visits were possible.

Social-vulnerability assessment uses the living conditions of the communities in a given region as trace indicators, on the basis that these reflect not just the resources available to these communities, but also their degree of marginalisation and exclusion from social, economic, and political systems. It thus provides us with a clear link between the two focuses of emergencies and development, in that the degree of vulnerability of a given community is a consequence of that community's level of inclusion in or exclusion from the general model of development. In fact, the reduction of vulnerability belongs under the heading of 'development' rather than in the category of 'emergencies' as it is conventionally conceived.

The study also deals with the differing levels of vulnerability of women and men. The trace indicators of living conditions are differentiated by sex whenever the statistics and collected studies allow for this. Other fundamental elements that demonstrate the differing levels of vulnerability of men and women are also covered, such as female poverty, the proportion of families headed by women, and their state of health and nutrition. Similarly, the participation of women in social organisations is considered, because this in itself facilitates or limits their access to emergency resources. Also studied is the participation of women in rural agricultural production.

To summarise, we assume that at a regional level vulnerability can be measured by the current living conditions of a threatened group, which varies according to sectors (rural/urban, women/men), and the probability that a given occurrence (threat) will outstrip their capacity for survival and meeting their basic needs. The following factors have been considered.

- **The level of poverty,** which in itself indicates that families have severely limited resources and precarious survival conditions, particularly when they are living in conditions of extreme poverty. Associated with and resulting from extreme poverty are all the other characteristics of vulnerability (such as low level of schooling, lack of basic services, inadequate housing), because the level of poverty expresses the productivity of the family, whether measured by the extent to which a family can meet their basic needs or by the poverty line (capacity to access basic staples, given a determined level of family income). The more precarious the family's capacity for survival, the more fragile their productivity in the face of external factors.

- **The standard of health** (mortality, morbidity). Although this is in itself related to overall levels of poverty, it expresses the degree of hygiene and sanitation of the community and the probability and risk of epidemics or death during and after a disaster or emergency.

- **The level of malnutrition** is used to indicate the degree of food security of a given community. Levels for women and girls are considered separately, as they tend to be the most vulnerable to malnutrition. If there is high overall malnutrition, food shortages in an emergency put women and girls in an even more precarious situation, causing starvation and even death.

- **The proportion of households headed by women,** and their level of poverty. The level of vulnerability of these households is shown by the fact that their probability of survival in the event of an emergency is less, since they have limited access to services and resources, including the benefits of development programmes. Their participation in the community and in co-operatives, through which resources are channelled in emergencies, is also limited.

- **The level of illiteracy,** which also varies according to sex. This is in itself an indicator of marginalisation and is a decisive factor in the community's access to information, services, and resources in every sense, including in emergency situations.

- **Living conditions,** where vulnerability is commonly seen in overcrowding and the precarious structure of housing. These factors allow us to determine the degree of protection or weakness, should a threat occur.

Two prevailing factors on government agendas across the region also tend to increase the vulnerability of communities at risk: economic structural adjustment and poverty.

Structural adjustment policies have two common factors with a negative impact: first, monetary policies, which cause rural production to slow down and urban unemployment to grow, resulting in greater numbers of unemployed and impoverished people, living in insecure conditions in both cities and the countryside; and, second, reductions in social spending in order to bring down fiscal deficits and public expenditure, which affect the poorest the most. Despite the modernisation of the state that is supposed to accompany structural adjustment, there has been reluctance and resistance on the part of central government to decentralise and to strengthen local and municipal government.

These local authorities ought to be the principal agents in articulating local development efforts and strengthening the capacity of communities and individuals for preparedness, prevention, and mitigation in the event of disasters. But there is no real tradition of local government in the region, except in the capital and major cities of each country. Elsewhere local government is effectively an institutional reference point without resources or decision-making capacity. If this system is maintained, vulnerability in affected zones will progressively increase.

The connections between poverty and vulnerability are clear. In the last 20 years the region has been exposed to various situations arising from the prevailing economic and political structures, for example the economic crisis facing highly dependent economies, the exacerbation of armed conflicts, and the impact of structural adjustment. The combined effects have resulted in migration, both internally and externally, an increase in the levels of unemployment and poverty, and the growing exclusion of broad sectors of the population from access to goods and basic services.

As can be seen from Table 4, every country has registered increasing levels of poverty and of extreme poverty. Even in the case of Costa Rica, where the overall level has stayed the same, the increase in extreme poverty is worrying. Given the continuation of programmes of structural adjustment and the economic changes brought about by globalisation, the trend has been one of greater deterioration, principally because of the increase in extreme poverty, as economic policies cause even greater exclusion of the poor in rural and marginal urban areas.

Table 4: Poverty in Mexico and Central America

Country	% living in poverty 1980	1991	Extreme poverty 1980	1991
Costa Rica	27.3	27.7	13.6	18.5
El Salvador	70.2	75.4	51.1	52.3
Guatemala	63.8	75.8	31.5	52.2
Honduras	67.6	76.5	56.8	62.7
Nicaragua	63.8	74.4	33.3	41.8
Mexico	44.9	59.9	10.0	no data

Female poverty and above all the feminisation of poverty are complex topics, and it is not the intention of this study to enter into an exhaustive discussion of them. It aims rather to indicate certain factors, so that the differing conditions experienced by impoverished women and men can be seen. About 25 per cent of households in the region are headed by women, because of the death of the spouse in conflict, or abandonment, or the spouse's migration for political or economic reasons. The figures for Nicaragua and Honduras are especially high, at 36 per cent and 27 per cent respectively. The importance of ensuring a gender perspective in emergency programmes is evident here, particularly if the distribution of, for example, food is carried out through the male head of the family, which in many cases means that fatherless households are excluded. There are exceptionally high levels of poverty within these households. In Honduras, for example, 72 per cent of families headed by women live in extreme poverty, compared with a figure of 63 per cent overall.

The feminisation of poverty in the region is only partly demonstrated by the differences in levels of poverty experienced by men and women. It is also seen in the *degree* of the poverty experienced, and the greater difficulties confronting women when they try to escape from this condition. The inequalities in opportunity in, for example, education, employment, pay (Table 6), ownership, and credit severely marginalise women and trap them in poverty. When adversity strikes, their survival is even more precarious, because of inequalities even in access to humanitarian aid.

On average, women in Central America earn almost 25 per cent less than men do for equal work. There are also differences in levels of literacy, the greatest difference being in Guatemala, where 48 per cent of women are illiterate, compared with 34 per cent of men. In Costa Rica, Panama, and Nicaragua, levels of male and female illiteracy are almost the same. However, the overall picture changes substantially when the same figures are broken down by sector (rural/urban or indigenous population). For example, 36 per cent of indigenous men in Panama are illiterate, whereas for women the figure is approaching 53 per cent. In short, Central American women experience above-average conditions of marginalisation and poverty.

32

Table 5: Families headed by women

	Mexico	Guatemala	El Salvador	Honduras	Nicaragua	Costa Rica	Panama
Families headed by women*	18%	22%	No data	27%	36%	23%	25%
% living in extreme poverty**	no data	No data	No data	72%	No data	12%	49%

* in urban areas, 1990
** on average (rural–urban)

Table 6: Women's earnings as a proportion of men's earnings, 1990, and corresponding levels of illiteracy

	Mexico		Guatemala		Honduras		Nicaragua		Panama		El Salvador	
% of male salary earned by women	76%		77%		77%		No data		77%		No data	
	M	F	M	F	M	F	M	F	M	F	M	F
Male and female illiteracy	10%	15%	34%	48%	24%	29%	23%	24%	10%	11%	24%	30%

Female participation in agriculture

The participation of women in agricultural production in Central America has been used as an indicator to measure vulnerability, because emergencies also have an impact on female production, causing losses, for example in produce grown on the *solar* or family plot. As women's contribution to production becomes clear, particularly its role in assuring food security for the family, so does the need to devise and implement emergency programmes which salvage their production as well as that of men, and restore the losses caused by droughts, floods, hurricanes, and other disasters.

On average, between 60 per cent and 84 per cent of women in Central America contribute to the production of basic grains through their work on rural small-holdings; between 70 per cent and 90 per cent help to farm cattle. Nicaragua, El Salvador, Honduras, and Panama are the countries where the most cattle-farming takes place (IICA 1996).

Women are also responsible for tending the family plot, growing vegetables and fruit trees, and poultry farming. All these tasks contribute to the food security of the family, as this produce is eaten by the family members themselves and is the main source of variety in their diet. When disasters strike, causing losses in food produced at home, they put the food security of the family in direct jeopardy. If humanitarian aid is to re-establish food security and restore production, resources must be directly targeted at these household economies.

Often the income deriving from such economies, although not great, is more stable than the income from men's agricultural production, because women's production is more varied and is less affected by national or international markets. In times of crisis, or when there are severe production shortages on the small-holding, the very survival of the family depends on what is produced by women. It is precisely the vegetables and fruit grown at home and the poultry raised in the yard that make continued survival possible.

Indigenous peoples

Throughout the region live indigenous communities who maintain their traditional

33

ways of life, culture, and governance. In Mexico and Guatemala, they form a large part of the demographic composition (13 per cent and 49 per cent respectively). In Honduras, El Salvador, and Nicaragua the proportion varies between 4 per cent and 7 per cent of the total population. (In the areas where these communities are concentrated, however, they may be the majority or sole ethnic group.) The needs of indigenous populations are highly relevant to emergency work, because the areas where they live are also those which are at very high risk.

The indigenous communities are highly marginalised and hence exhibit high levels of poverty. This is because they lack resources and access to services, and because of their geographical inaccessibility, which is a product of their exclusion from prevailing socio-economic systems. If we add to this their marginalisation from established channels of expression, and hence from participating in making decisions that affect their lives, we can see that they are left very vulnerable in the event of disasters. It is precisely this level of exclusion that has led many of these groups in Guatemala, Mexico, and Nicaragua in particular to strengthen their organisational structures. Some have even entered into conflict with the dominant groups to find and express solutions to their needs.

Progressive rural exclusion and increasingly vulnerable cities

The population of the region has become increasingly urbanised. Unlike the urbanisation of the 1960s and 1970s, which was caused by processes of industrialisation, the latest phase is the result of displacement because of war and the increasingly precarious rural economy. As a result of this mass displacement, cities and towns in the region house huge numbers of the now urban poor, in settlements where the living conditions, lack of basic services, and unemployment all increase their vulnerability.

The disasters of the greatest magnitude occur along the highly populated Pacific coastline, and the majority of the urban poor of the region have suffered sudden volcanic eruptions, earthquakes, and landslides.

Guatemala, Honduras, Nicaragua, and El Salvador all register high annual levels of growth in the urban population (4.0, 4.7, 4.1, and 3.6 per cent respectively), which will continue to rise as young people are forced out of deprived rural areas and have no alternative but to move to the cities. These young migrants increase the levels of urban poverty, which is further aggravated by the fact that none of the countries has any plans for urban development. Precarious settlements continue to spread chaotically, with bad use of land. These settlements generally have no services and face great risks, as they are situated on hillsides, are structurally unsound, and are built with inadequate materials.

While increased urbanisation has meant that the rural population has decreased, war across wide areas of the countryside, and now structural adjustment have led to increasing marginalisation and poverty in rural areas. What is more, the contraction and slowing down of the agricultural export industry, owing to the crisis in international prices, has created widespread unemployment in rural areas,

Table 7: Proportion of the population of Central America living in poverty

Country	Urban sector % Population		% Poverty		Rural sector % Population		% Poverty		Deforestation	
	1980	1990	1980	1990	1980	1990	1980	1990	1000s hectares	% year
Costa Rica	46.0	53.6	17	19	54.0	46.4	33.3	38.8	50.0	3.1
El Salvador	41.5	47.7	58	63	58.5	52.3	76.9	84.9	5.0	3.2
Guatemala	38.5	42.0	66	67	61.5	58.0	66.7	86.1	90.0	2.0
Honduras	35.9	43.6	44	61	64.1	56.4	67.5	79.3	80.0	2.3
Nicaragua	53.4	59.6	46	56	46.6	40.4	76.9	87.8	100.0	2.7

where incomes depend on permanent or seasonal work. Moreover, structural adjustment measures have curtailed the aid and credit programmes that supported the fragile economies of small and medium-sized producers and have reduced them to subsistence level. Cuts in public spending, principally on education and health care, have also had a fundamental impact on the rural population, whose access to these services is increasingly limited.

All the Central American countries have shown an increase in rural poverty, with Guatemala and Honduras reflecting this most drastically. The rural areas have also suffered disasters, both natural and conflict-related. Wide areas fluctuate between flooding and drought, with conditions exacerbated by the high level of deforestation, in areas where soil and woodland have not been properly managed. The degradation of soil, woodland, and water resources also means that the productivity of small and medium-sized farms will be reduced.

Inadequate housing

The day-to-day living conditions and hygiene of the majority of families in the region, which are a product of chronic poverty, are the most crucial factors in evaluating their level of protection or vulnerability in the face of disasters. Nearly one third of families lack access to services like clean drinking water. The situation is even more serious in rural areas, where, with the exception of Costa Rica, all the countries show alarming deficiencies. Services

for sewage disposal are similarly lacking, and even more disturbingly a large number of urban households are not connected to sewage systems, but have latrines.

There is serious over-crowding and inadequate housing infrastructure, for example walls made of *bahareque* (mud and wattle) or wood, and earth floors. A very high proportion of households use wood-stoves. In addition, settlements have not been planned, but have grown organically as poor families have migrated or resettled, which is the reason for the proliferation of improvised houses on hillsides and in high-risk locations. These people are more greatly exposed to earthquakes and the collapse of the hillsides around the edges of towns.

With the exception of Costa Rica, all the countries have continued to build up an increasing housing deficit, which is becoming ever more difficult to resolve. Indeed, the problem is being aggravated by the influx of rural migrants and by people moving house within cities, putting great pressure on urban land. This has often resulted in clashes and violence, and the press reports people being forcibly evicted on a daily basis, with no alternative accommodation provided for them by their governments.

The collapse of the slopes of the San Salvador volcano in 1982, which occurred as a result of a combination of heavy rains and deforestation, serves as a good illustration: 50 people living in the precarious settlements on the slopes died, 2,400 people were injured, 120 houses were completely destroyed, and losses suffered by other households were estimated at US$0.5m.

Table 8: Hygiene and living conditions

Country	Access to clean drinking water %				Access to sanitation %		% Using firewood	Over-Crowding	Weak infra structure
	1980	1991	Urban	Rural	Urban	Rural			
Costa Rica	72	92	85	99	100	94	33	11.6	No data
El Salvador	53	57	78	38	91	65	46	52.7	75.8
Guatemala	39	64	92	43	72	52	57	56.7	No data
Honduras	41	67	81	53	96	61	62	64	No data
Nicaragua	46	60	81	23	77	34	70	53.6	46.0
Mexico	62	77	90	66	81	29	no data	57	35

Disasters and health

Although official health statistics record a slight improvement in the principal indicators, with the exception of Costa Rica (where there is an almost universal system of health care) only a fraction of the population is covered by public health services (Table 9). Central America continues to be the region of Latin America where the general health status of the population has deteriorated most severely. It should be noted that this information shows national or regional averages, not sufficiently refined to show the inequalities or gaps in the service that affect different socio-economic groups, or differentials between women and men.

Table 9: Rates of infant and maternal mortality

Country	Infant mortality	Mortality under 5 years old	Maternal mortality per 10,000 live births
Costa Rica	14	16	4
El Salvador	42	56	14
Guatemala	60	70	22
Honduras	49	54	22
Nicaragua	56	68	15
Mexico	36	no data	6

Source: FLACSO, 1995

Throughout Central America (bar Costa Rica), rates of infant mortality are increasing. In Mexico, the infant mortality rate has fallen. The causes of death are similar, with intestinal infections the principal factor, followed by respiratory infections, with malnutrition contributing to some 85 per cent of infant deaths. This situation is clearly associated with poverty (poor diet, water, sanitation, schooling, etc.) and also reflects the restricted access of poorer communities to these services (see Table 10).

Although the rates are highest in rural areas, coinciding with patterns for the distribution of poverty, it is also true that the urban rates do not reflect the true situation exactly. This was demonstrated by a study carried out in Managua in 1991 (UNICEF-MINSA), where, when the deaths were grouped according to the level of schooling of the mother, the death rate of the children of illiterate urban women was 101 per 1,000 live births, while that of the children of illiterate rural women was 79 per 1,000 live births. With the exception of accidents as a cause of death in the under-fives, the pattern in countries with a high death rate is the same in this group as for infants, i.e. the cause of death is linked to poverty and marginalisation.

Maternal mortality rates have also increased, even allowing for the under-registration of deaths in this category through inadequate classification systems. These deaths are associated with a lack of health care before and during the birth. This shows not only the level of marginalisation of a large part of the population from services, and their lack of access for geographical or economic reasons, but also a culture of widespread rejection of and lack of confidence in these services. Moreover, it shows the low priority accorded to the maternal and

Table 10: Causes of infant mortality

Infant mortality%	Costa Rica	El Salvador	Guatemala	Honduras	Nicaragua	Mexico
Intestinal infections	15	50	57	61	4	7.9
Respiratory infections	8	35	37	37	28	13.3
Perinatal causes	13	19	24	15	19	43.3
Illnesses preventable by immunisation	0	10	14	16	4	2
Under-nourishment	1	7	7	4	6	2.7
Other causes	71	24	12	20	33	30.8

reproductive health of women, which is an expression of the gender discrimination inherent in the system.

There is a noticeably high rate of maternal mortality in Guatemala and Honduras, which both have a rate of 22 deaths per 10,000 live births, followed by Nicaragua with 15 per 10,000. It should however be noted that the national averages obscure differences across states or departments, and even between urban and rural areas. For example, a study of the state of Tlaxcala in Mexico found that the maternal mortality there was almost three times the national average, approaching 19 per 10,000 live births.

The health services in the region have deteriorated in recent years (see Table 11), principally because of fiscal policy and cuts in social spending. Only in Costa Rica and El Salvador has the ratio of inhabitants per doctor improved. Reform of health services has begun with budget cuts, resulting not only in the closure

of peripheral health centres but also in the introduction of charges in mobile clinics and in hospitals. Resources and qualified personnel are concentrated in urban centres, while private health services, which mainly cover urban areas, have increased. Most public services suffer from permanent shortages of countless essentials and equipment.

All this paints a picture of a situation in which health services have a reduced capacity to meet the growing demands of a population that is more exposed than ever to the risk of disease and death, as a result of everyday living conditions. Vulnerability, which is already high, is increasing because of the current political climate.

Malnutrition and under-nourishment

A crucial aspect in determining the vulnerability of communities is their degree of food security (Table 12). Evidently poverty and unemployment

Table 11: Health services in the region

Health services	Costa Rica	El Salvador	Guatemala	Honduras	Nicaragua	Mexico
Inhabitants/Doctor 1980	1.473	2.860	1.773	2.945	2.067	1.081
Inhabitants/Doctor 1990	1.136	1.563	4.000	3.130	1.670	1.850
Beds/1000 inhabitants 1980	3.0	1.3	1.8	1.4	1.7	0.8
Beds/1000 inhabitants 1990	2.2	1.1	1.1	1.1	1.3	0.7
% Hospital births	97	66	23	63	42	45

Table 12: Dietary and nutritional conditions

Country	Food production 1980 = 100	Food imported 1980 = 100	Calorie intake	Acute infant under-nourishment	Under-weight at birth	Under-nourished mothers (index of body weight)
Costa Rica	104	72	100	6	6	no data
El Salvador	95	123	78	13	11	9.1
Guatemala	94	109	78	34	14	13.9
Honduras	89	118	70	19	9	18.2
Nicaragua	64	123	77	12	12	10.4
Mexico	no data	180	100	14	5	no data

determine the level of consumption and nutrition of a household. This is even more the case when the purchasing power of the salaries of those in work provides no guarantees. Starting with a value of 100 in 1980, the only country that has maintained that level of salary is Honduras (99.9 per cent). As for the rest of the countries, in some the level has been moderately reduced, for example in Costa Rica (to 86.7 per cent of the former value) and Guatemala (78.4 per cent), and in others it has been drastically reduced, for example in El Salvador (to 34 per cent) and Nicaragua (to 12.4 per cent).

Evidently families have developed survival strategies which range from participating in the growth of the informal urban sector (principally in commercial activities), to prostitution, delinquency, and, in the last few years, migration. This has not only sustained families in receipt of payments but has also provided one of the main sources of income for countries, principally El Salvador (around US$1.2m, or double the value of exports), Guatemala and Nicaragua (about US$350m a year, equivalent to the total value of exports). In these three countries, families in receipt of this income spend it almost exclusively on food (82 per cent or more), so it can be assumed that it provides the sole or most important source of income for these families.

In addition, structural adjustment programmes have further restricted support for agricultural production, except in the export industry. This has caused food production to slow down and increased the amount of food imported and the degree of food dependency. Costa Rica is the only country where production is increasing and imports decreasing. As a result, there are deficiencies in terms of calorie intake, and apart from Costa Rica and Mexico (despite their greater dependency) food consumption in all the countries is apparently well below the necessary level. Levels of acute under-nutrition (weight/height) in children are very high, as is stunting of growth, seen in 35–50 per cent of school-age children. The number of underweight births continues to be widely under-recorded, as figures tell only of births in health-care institutions, i.e. a very low proportion. Even so, the rate is high, reflecting not only the vulnerability of the infant but also the degree of under-nutrition of mothers, seen also in the index of body weight.

This all means that the degree of vulnerability, although defined according to the risk of a given threat, is essentially determined by levels of marginalisation and exclusion, which are directly related to patterns of economic growth and the political and social organisation of a country. It is not sheer coincidence that the most deprived areas and communities in the region have been the sites and protagonists of the conflicts that raged in the 1980s, nor that they have suffered when natural disasters have struck. A cycle of poverty, conflict, and recurrent loss of lives and resources as a result of emergencies has developed, which has weakened people's capacity to participate in an on-going process of sustainable human development. In each cycle things are gained and then lost as circumstances fluctuate, and in the majority of cases survival merely means starting again in a worse condition, ready to begin the next cycle.

The living conditions of vulnerable groups are deteriorating in contrast with the general trends in the economies of the countries in the region. On the whole, the countries of the region are demonstrating increasingly better health standards, while the poor, the indigenous peoples, women, and children — the great majority — all remain extremely vulnerable in the face of the risks to which they are exposed. Natural disasters and conflicts have always affected the poorest people most, and Mexico and Central America are no exception. The livelihoods and resources lost in the many disasters that have occurred have rarely been recuperated. The same areas and groups affected in the past are those that are still exposed to the greatest risks today, in situations of high and increasing vulnerability.

To sum up, the entire region is exposed to a high risk in the face of all types of threat, but the most vulnerable groups are those living in the areas that also show the greatest levels of poverty, and, with the exception of Costa Rica, which has managed to improve its living standards, the link between poverty and vulnerability remains a constant and a challenge.

A country-by-country view of social vulnerability

This section aims to give a basic overview of the communities facing the greatest levels of risks in the event of emergencies, and to describe the general conditions prevailing in zones categorised as 'high risk' in Mexico, Guatemala, El Salvador, Honduras, and Nicaragua.

Mexico

The two areas of Mexico categorised as 'high risk' are the central region, comprising 10 states covering the most densely populated area of the country, including the Federal District (metropolitan area), and the south, including the states of Chiapas, Oaxaca, and Veracruz. In reality, the two zones are fairly homogeneous in terms of their overall social vulnerability. The central region is well known for its social inequalities, while the south contains three of Mexico's five most marginalised states. The whole of the south registers average levels of poverty which are far greater than those in the rest of the country. The high proportion of poor housing without running water or sanitation is also well known. Over-crowding, although it occurs principally in the south, is fairly generalised in the country. Within the central zone, the states of Guerrero, Hidalgo, and Puebla are classified as the third, fourth, and sixth most marginalised states in Mexico.

Although the situation seems to be better in the Federal District, which comes last in terms of its degree of marginalisation (in 32nd place), the impression is illusory. Just a tiny percentage increase in the already more than 10m inhabitants who face high risks and vulnerabilities would be enough to equal the number in other states. What should be emphasised, however, is the high risk of earthquakes, volcanic eruptions (Popocatépetl), and landslides in precarious settlements.

Within the two high-risk zones, different groups face differing degrees of vulnerability:

- the indigenous populations who represent 36 per cent of the total population in the state of Oaxaca, 25 per cent in Chiapas, 17 per cent in Hidalgo, 13 per cent in Puebla, and 10 per cent in Veracruz;
- the marginalised rural and urban populations in the entire area;
- the population around Popocatépetl.

Within these groups, indigenous people and women in general are more vulnerable, particularly where families are without fathers, as shown by the indicators of health status prevailing among them.

As the WHO/PAHO report of 1996 indicates, infectious diseases deriving from insanitary conditions, malnutrition, and poverty are not among the six primary overall causes of death in Mexico. However, among the five primary causes of death in the indigenous population are preventable intestinal infections and respiratory diseases, including diarrhoea, influenza, and pneumonia, as well as measles. The sixth most common cause of death among indigenous people is malnutrition, which appears in twelfth place for the Mexican population overall; indeed the death rate for the indigenous population is 1.3 times that of the global figure for Mexico.

There is considerable malnutrition, particularly among women. In rural areas, it affects one-fifth of all women of child-bearing age (OPS/PAHO 1994), with nutritional and metabolic difficulties constituting the second-commonest cause of female mortality. At the same time, at least 17 per cent of Mexican households are headed by women, and female illiteracy stands at 63 per cent.

Table 13: Vulnerability among Mexican women

Illiteracy	15% of women are illiterate (63% of the total incidence of illiteracy in Mexico)
3 principal causes of female mortality	1. Circulatory illnesses 2. Nutritional and metabolic problems 3. Tumours
Maternal mortality	6.1 per 10,000 live births (under-registered)
Households headed by women	17.3% (approximately 3 million)

Source: Elu, 1996 and FLACSO, 1993

In the highly marginalised states in question, infant mortality is as high as 1.5 times the national average. The causes are the same as those resulting from poverty and exclusion (intestinal and respiratory infections, malnutrition, etc.). These states also have the highest fertility rates (with an average of more than five children per woman). In states where there are lower levels of marginalisation, the causes of infant mortality are mainly perinatal or congenital. The same is true of maternal mortality (although the figures are distorted through under-registration). Moreover, the differences between states are considerable. A study in the state of Tlaxcala found a rate of maternal mortality of 19.8 per 10,000 live births, three times the national average (Elu 1996).

Popocatépetl

The conditions and degrees of vulnerability described above are also generally found in the urban communities threatened by Popocatépetl, in settlements which have the same high degree of unmet basic needs as those in rural areas. This pattern appears across a series of communities which are relatively widely dispersed, and where the population is largely concentrated in urban areas. These communities are living in high-risk zones, according to the mapping carried out by SINAPROC, and their vulnerability is greater than their socio-economic conditions might suggest, because of the high degree of political polarisation.

In Tlamanalco, for instance, most people are aged between 12 and 24 years. Some of these young people are involved in business and service industries, but a large proportion are unemployed and so forced to seek alternatives in the informal sector, despite the good agricultural land. Consequently, people are very dependent on cash income and the market for their food security. The production of maize and beans for family consumption takes place alongside the production of and trade in flowers and fruit. Women work principally in buying and selling the latter. Few families have cattle and sheep. These are good sources of food and income but, as is the case with agriculture, livestock is easily affected by volcanic activity, with a great risk of losses to families who, because of their level of poverty, would be unable to recover them. Approximately one-quarter of the population here actually live in the USA, the majority of whom are men. This leaves a similar proportion of women who are the *de facto* sole heads of families. The men's monthly remittance is one of the principal sources of income and therefore of food security for these women and their families.

Living in other communities are Nahuatl, Otomi, Zapotec, Mazahua, and Mixtec indigenous people, who, like other ethnic minorities, are marginalised and have little access to basic services like health care and education, which are generally concentrated in the main towns. The situation in Tlamanalco provides one such example: there are nine districts, but only two of them are served by doctors, even then with a ratio of one doctor per 20,000 inhabitants. This seriously restricts the medical attention given in the frequent cases of respiratory illnesses, chickenpox, measles, and intestinal infections, which are among the principal causes of death.

In terms of infrastructure and services, at least in the case of Tlamanalco and to some extent in

other municipalities visited (Almecameca, Ecatzingo, Atlautla), there are postal services, telephones, and electricity. However, the telephones (so important in an emergency situation) do not work. Local people explain that they 'were installed for political reasons, not to solve the communication problems of the community'. The main access road to the communities at risk is relatively good, but secondary roads are affected by great cracks which have developed at the foot of the volcano. This increases the vulnerability of groups living away from the main road, because it would be almost impossible to evacuate them in the event of an emergency.

In terms of the organisation and cohesion of the people in the communities concerning the risks they all face, there are difficulties in co-ordination which have been caused by widespread political polarisation, resulting from the fact that the opposition has taken control of various municipalities since the last elections. This fact is also relevant at other levels, in view of the fact that SINAPROC also works in a very centralised way, and it is possible that in the event of an emergency it might not prioritise assistance to the communities administered by the opposition. This struggle for political power increases the high levels of vulnerability of the threatened population.

There are other important elements concerning preparedness for disaster response. In Tlamanalco, there are only three civil protection agents. They have given some talks in schools and to specific audiences, but do not have the capacity to address the needs of the population. In Ecatzingo, a town in the first ring of risk, there is only one civil protection agent, which is obviously unable to develop a preparedness strategy in a responsible way. The picture is similar in the neighbouring communities.

The lack of CSOs concerned with the problem of the volcano is well known. Those that do exist are more interested in doing research — for example UNAM, which has carried out geo-dynamic studies to determine probable scenarios for volcanic activity. However, there are practically no organisations developing strategies for prevention and preparedness. This is possibly due to the fact that the state has developed policies exclusively through SINAPROC. Whatever the reason, this lack of organisations has repercussions on the communities, reducing the probability that they will receive help in a crisis.

Chiapas: politics and low-intensity war

The prolonged suspension of dialogue between the federal government of Mexico and the Zapatista National Liberation Army (EZLN) has seriously jeopardised the peace process. In December 1996, the government rejected a legislative proposal drawn up by the commission created to assist with the peace process, that the San Andrés accords on Indigenous Rights and Culture should be implemented. The government insists that its own alternative proposal is consistent with the peace accords, although many observers disagree and accuse the government of breaking the accords and deliberately undermining the peace process.

The Peace Conciliation Commission (COCOPA) insists that its proposal, which was presented to the parties as an ultimatum after months of talks, should be upheld. However, in March 1997, COCOPA declared ambiguously that 'the text could be improved' and declined to present it to Congress without the support of the Executive. The EZLN continues to demand certain minimum conditions for the peace talks to resume and is reluctant to negotiate new terms while the existing accords remain incomplete.

Meanwhile, a new wave of violence in Chiapas has once again drawn public attention to the stagnant peace process and the increasing instability of the state. In the northern zone, which is under siege, paramilitary groups have imposed a repressive regime on some areas, resulting in confrontations, murders, robberies, and displacement of people from their homes. A number of events, such as land disputes, have served as major flash-points for confrontations and for the arrest and torture of innocent people. The impunity enjoyed by the security forces and the paramilitary groups, and the discriminatory treatment that is meted out to indigenous people who do not support the ruling party are all evidence of grave deficiencies in the administration of justice.

An increased military presence in Chiapas and other states where there has been conflict, including parts of Mexico City, has reinforced the fear that the government is leaning towards a military rather than a political solution, and is employing a strategy of low-intensity war. In a situation of such great tension, with little hope of progress in the negotiations and with troops attacking and even killing communities who sympathise with the EZLN, the ceasefire seems increasingly fragile. The continuation of fighting may also tarnish the government's credibility both within Mexico and internationally, especially in the wake of the critical judgements of the Inter-American Human Rights Commission and the UN Committee for the Elimination of Racial Discrimination.

The involvement of Mexican civil society in the peace process has been fundamental to its progress to date, with an *Encuentro Nacional por la Paz* (National Assembly for Peace) having involved 91 organisations in 19 states. The influence that international economic interests could have on developments in the Chiapas conflict underlines the importance of the international community making an active and far-reaching commitment to the search for a fair and lasting peace.

Various factors related to the conflict are having an influence on the levels of risks and vulnerability. Among these are militarisation, food insecurity, poor health, and forced migration.

Militarisation: In the last three years the military presence in Chiapas has increased from 5,000 soldiers to 75,000, with negative consequences for the economic, social, political, and environmental life of the local communities.

- An artificial economy prevails, due to the (unsustainable) demand for services, which women are largely expected to meet. This is putting great pressure on local resources and aggravating the socio-environmental crisis, principally in terms of food and firewood. The demand for services like laundry, fetching wood and water, and the preparation of tortillas and other food has increased women's workload and diminished their capacity to attend to the needs of their own families.

- The high level of prostitution is a response to the military presence and the economic impact of the conflict on the population. Women have been forced to offer sexual services for money, and parents have obliged their daughters to prostitute themselves to create a source of income. This surge in prostitution is also linked to the lack of viable opportunities for women to earn money, which is in itself a consequence of inadequacies in the aid systems, including social and productive projects.

- The feeble economies of these communities have been strongly affected by the military presence. Animal grazing has been curtailed for reasons of security, and wool production, which represents an important source of household income, has declined.

41

- Responsibility for looking after the home, supporting the family economically, and keeping the community together is falling more and more to women, given that the men have either had to emigrate or must meet military obligations to their communities. In some areas, for example Los Altos (which comprises 22 municipalities and 2,000 communities), the burden of family and community responsibilities has fallen to women and girls. Women have become the *de facto* heads of their households, and their work has become the principal source of family income. This area is also affected by drought, which intensifies the already high degree of vulnerability of these families.

- Health standards, especially in the zones where most fighting has taken place, have seriously deteriorated. Psychosomatic illnesses are now frequent, especially in women, who are under great pressure, face harassment and abuse, and have to bear the emotional burden of knowing that they and their families are in constant danger.

- The presence of soldiers in the community has resulted in intimidation, fear, and psychological pain. It prevents women from going freely about their work and their daily business, and restricts their access to services. It has also caused an increase in alcoholism and drug addiction, especially among young people. The military cynically use this as a pretext for their presence, claiming that they are needed to ensure 'the rule of law'.

- The cutting down of trees in conservation areas is a consequence of the militarisation, the effects of which cannot be measured in the short term but will certainly have a great impact in the future.

- Production has been drastically reduced. Vegetable plots, for example, have had to be abandoned because of continuous alarms.

- The effects of a 'militarised culture' extend beyond the present day and will affect future generations.

Forced migration: Forced migration is an important risk factor in conflicts. It involves individuals and communities being uprooted and displaced, as well as people returning to their former homes. It is estimated that more than 5,000 families in Chiapas are currently undergoing some form of forced displacement, the majority as a result of inter-community conflicts (provoked by para-militaries) and land disputes.

This is a problem that has only just begun to appear on the agenda of local organisations. Hence there is no expertise in the area, and follow-up in conflict situations has not been systematic, making it difficult to obtain detailed information on the communities affected. The most significant migrations are occurring in the northern zone towards the centre of the region and Tuxtla Gutiérrez (the state capital), and from the border area to neighbouring zones.

Recently displacement has been occurring with great frequency, apparently as part of a wider military strategy; some 20,000 people are directly affected. Summary displacements take place without people being given the chance to gather together the bare necessities for subsistence. Typically, the evictions are associated with rape, the burning down of houses, and the destruction of crops. In one incident witnessed by us in the course of the mapping exercise, the community did not have time to gather together even basic belongings or food for the children. Families were left on the streets, with only their dogs and their resolve to return to reclaim their land once the BOM (the Joint Operations Brigade) had withdrawn.

Displaced and returning families are highly vulnerable. Having lost their homes and often having to relocate in a place where they are not able to do their normal work, they have no resources with which to re-start their lives. They need housing materials, tools, cooking utensils, medicines, food, and seeds. There is an urgent need for local organisations to be helped to develop an assistance strategy.

Food insecurity: Food insecurity currently threatens about 1.5 million people in Chiapas. The problem is becoming increasingly acute because of the conflict, and also because of drought and marked environmental degradation. Food insecurity is caused by a combination of factors.

- Land insecurity and lack of access to land.

- Restricted food supplies, because of the strong military presence and the actions of paramilitary groups. The troops' demand for food is causing food supplies to run out and shortages of basic products in Chiapas.

- Lack of income for rural families.

- Moderate to severe droughts which are occurring frequently in the state, especially in the highlands and in the Sierra of Motozintla. Drought is ultimately one of the most critical factors in food insecurity, along with deteriorating quality of soil.

• Restrictions on the freedom of movement of women, as a result of insecurity and violence against them, which affect the economy and the food security of the family. For example, female shepherds have stopped taking their lambs and goats to graze in the fields.

• The same situation limits women's access to markets, crops, water and firewood, making daily subsistence more difficult, especially since 90 per cent of homes use wood or charcoal for cooking. The troops get their water supplies from the rivers where women collect their water and wash clothes.

• The soldiers take, sometimes by force, the food grown in the allotments and plots belonging to women, they steal their livestock and eggs as well as maize from the fields, and even raid their belongings, including household utensils. Food security is even more threatened in the zones where there is drought.

• There are high levels of female malnutrition. Social services such as school breakfasts and milk have been withdrawn in some regions, making the nutritional situation even worse for girls.

Faced with the problem of food insecurity, communities are very vulnerable. Solutions require a combination of emergency and development programmes, and should be focused on areas where the stability of the population would ensure some success.

Health: Official statistics are unreliable, and tend to under-estimate the scale of the problem. Some of the following information is therefore based on the observations of health workers who were interviewed.

The average rate of infant mortality in the indigenous population is between 55 and 65 deaths per 1,000 live births. Chiapas has the highest level of maternal mortality in Mexico: 9 per 1,000 inhabitants, according to official statistics. One study carried out in the municipality of Chenalho, in Los Altos, placed maternal mortality among the two principal causes of death of women over a five-year period (1988–1993), along with diarrhoea and various intestinal infections. The same study found that of the 117 recorded female deaths between 10 and 49 years, 20 were directly related to maternity.

Anaemia, malnutrition, and complications related to pregnancy and childbirth represent the three principal problems in women's health. Others include parasites, diarrhoea, respiratory problems, skin diseases, and psychosomatic problems. There has also been a substantial increase in overall levels of social and family violence, and of sexual violence towards children and women since the militarisation and the intensification of the economic crisis. The rise in prostitution has resulted in an increase in sexually transmitted diseases and HIV/AIDS. Harassment, sexual abuse, and violence against women and children are also causing psychological problems, which are emerging in the form of widespread depressive and psychosomatic illnesses in Chiapas, especially in women and girls.

The government gives priority to family planning in its medical services for women (through distribution of contraceptives, but above all through sterilisation), which some NGOs think is a strategy for controlling population growth in Chiapas. Women who seek help for their daughters find themselves on the receiving end of family-planning campaigns, because staff in medical centres are obliged to promote this service to them.

Very little medical attention is available to women in other respects. There is a general lack of confidence in doctors and systems of health care, above all because the model of medical attention is culturally offensive to the mostly indigenous population, particularly women, who are largely monolingual and who find the doctors' approach and methods both demeaning and inappropriate. For most indigenous people, the only alternatives are the few health promoters and traditional midwives in their communities. Compounded by the restrictions on their freedom of movement, these conditions suggest that the great majority living in rural Chiapas lack access to health care.

Guatemala

Guatemala suffered 30 years of armed conflict, and the peace accords which ended it were signed only in December 1996. The last two decades, in particular, were very violent. Expressions of discontent with the political regime and social conditions were brutally repressed, paving the way for guerrilla movements from the early 1960s and the counter-insurgency programmes of successive military governments. From the mid-1970s, partly because of the impact of the earthquake of 1976, there was once again a strong surge of rebellion, this time also in urban areas, along with a strengthening of popular movements and an increasing presence and degree of organisation in other sectors of civil society. In response to this, from 1978 to 1982, one of the most repressive regimes in the history of Guatemala came into power. This regime isolated the country from the international community at the height of the economic crisis affecting Guatemala and the other Latin American nations. In the midst of an electoral fraud in 1982, institutional crisis, struggles within the army, and increasingly severe economic decline, Guatemala suffered several *coups d'état*. For four years, *de facto* military regimes were installed, espousing the new military creed of 'Security and Development' in the context of the army's counter-insurgency strategies: the result was that up to 70,000 people were murdered or 'disappeared'; more than 500 villages were totally destroyed; hundreds of thousands of people were displaced, and more than 10,000 sought refuge in other countries; 60,000 people were relocated to 'model villages' (strategic hamlets), and at least 500,000 had to live within 'development areas'. All this was accompanied by economic destruction and mass impoverishment, especially in the countryside: the worst catastrophe that the country has ever suffered.

Although after 1986 an 'opening up to democracy' was announced — a project designed by the army that allowed civil governments to be established through free elections — the corruption that characterised these elections caused a new political crisis. This culminated in the coup of May 1993, effected by the President of the Republic himself, and a new President was nominated by the Congress. The year 1994 was marked by political struggle between state powers, and elections for a new Congress were held. Barely 15 per cent of voters participated in them, demonstrating an enormous loss of confidence in the political system in Guatemala at that time. In short, the combination of increased political and economic deterioration during the first half of the 1980s and continuing armed conflict within the country exposed Guatemala — which already had high levels of poverty, marginalisation, and social polarisation, a lack of basic services, and an obsolete and inefficient institutional system — to unprecedented stresses.

As a result of the unsustainable situation in the country and external political and economic pressure, the peace accords were signed in December 1996. The major challenge now was to ensure that these accords were observed within a framework of democracy to ensure a firm and lasting peace. This marked a new era for the Guatemalan people, as the country emerged from disaster and entered a period of reconstruction.

The reconstruction began by ensuring that displaced communities were re-integrated into society, and among them 'the returned'. The process of return has, however, been long and slow. To date there are 34 returned communities, with more than 20 established in the former conflict areas, mainly in the Department of Quiché. The return process has encountered problems of access to land and resources; but, even with these difficulties to face, communities are determined to reintegrate. They have the support of various programmes and institutions to help them achieve this, in line with the conditions set out in the peace accords. In addition, on returning to the country, they have received a level of assistance from UNHCR (material, technical, and financial) which has put them in a better position than the rest of the population who stayed in Guatemala and bore the brunt of the cruelty and war. This disparity is in some cases causing difficulties between communities.

While in exile in Mexico, the refugees developed many skills and capacities and received a basic education. The women became organised, enrolled in literacy programmes, and managed various projects and other activities. It has proved hard for them to maintain these levels of leadership on returning to Guatemala. In many cases, their physical return has meant a return to their traditional roles, and their organisations and political activities have fallen by the wayside.

In this phase of rehabilitation and reconstruction, the communities who were displaced are of primary importance, among them groups who have returned, demobilised, been displaced internally, or repatriated, as they have an important role to play in rebuilding the social fabric of the country. These relocated communities are principally located in the western highlands, the north, central Petén, and the south-coast regions. About half of them live in Quiché. These zones have been identified as being at very high risk, because of both the threat of natural disasters (seismic and volcanic activity, floods, landslides, and droughts) and human factors, which are equally important. These areas have also suffered great environmental deterioration, with the highest levels of deforestation in the country, impoverished soil with alarming levels of deterioration of its capacity for production, and pollution of water sources by agro-chemicals. Unfortunately, female participation in the negotiations for the return was not very high, and this in part explains why the relocation sites are sometimes distant from sources of water or urban centres. Nor has it been easy for the communities to continue with their productive activities, since there are no commercial outlets or local markets, and they cannot obtain raw materials. For example, many of the former refugees know how to sew and how to make hammocks, but there is nowhere to buy thread, and no one to buy their products in any case. A return to basic subsistence farming is all they can rely on. All these geophysical, social, and economic factors place these communities at high risk.

If the overall socio-economic conditions prevailing in Guatemala are difficult, they are worse still among the displaced and relocated communities in the high-risk zones. Life expectancy is the lowest in Central America, at 63 years; the average rate of adult illiteracy is at least 43 per cent, but in rural areas it is approaching almost 72 per cent and in some places it is over 80 per cent. Illiteracy among women is the highest in Latin America. The proportion of children aged between 7 and 14 years who attend school is 63 per cent, but fewer than half of these manage to complete one or more levels of primary education, only nine per cent obtain a secondary level education, and hardly two per cent reach university level.

Only 3.3 per cent of the Guatemalan GNP is spent on health care, resulting in a situation where 46 per cent of the population has no access to any kind of medical attention. The health system covers only 25 per cent of the population, the social security institute a further 15 per cent, and the private sector 14 per cent. The ratio of hospital beds per person is 1/800, and half of the beds in public hospitals and four out of five beds in private hospitals are in the metropolitan area. These are the official figures: other sources indicate that only one in three Guatemalans has access to health services, given the calamitous state of public facilities. One study showed that more than one-third of users of official health services in rural areas had to travel 12km on average to reach the nearest facility (OPS/PAHO, 1996). This is more difficult for women, considering that their mobility is always more restricted by their responsibility for looking after the household and children.

Levels of malnutrition are very high, for example in schoolchildren aged between 6 and 9

years — not to mention the 37 per cent of children who do not attend school. Only 60 per cent of the population have access to clean drinking water. The consequences of the lack of health services, drinking water, and food are seen in the high rate of infant mortality. Of the total deaths registered in the country, more than 42 per cent are of children under the age of five.

Poverty has significantly increased and is growing at 5.3 per cent each year. In 1990, 63 per cent of households were living in poverty and 32 per cent in a state of extreme poverty. It is calculated that current figures have increased to 80 per cent and 55 per cent respectively, with the greatest levels of poverty concentrated in the central highlands. Urban poverty has also increased, and it is estimated that in the metropolitan area there are more than 800,000 people living in more than 240 precarious settlements. The proportion of the population that is economically active is the highest it has been for 10 years: of these, 55 per cent work in agriculture, 14 per cent in industry, 17 per cent in the service sector, and 14 per cent in the business sector. However, agriculture constitutes 25 per cent of national production, which indicates that most farmers practise subsistence farming: 2.2 per cent of Guatemala's landowners own 65 per cent of the country's fertile farm-land.

Population growth is one of the highest in Latin America, at 2.9 per cent p.a. The fertility rate is 5.9 children per woman of child-bearing age. Practically half of the population of Guatemala is aged less than 15, and the average age is 22 years. Almost 62 per cent of Guatemala's population live in rural areas, which makes it the country with the smallest urban population in Latin America. At the same time, 31 per cent of the population lives in the capital city and half in the department of Guatemala (the highest concentration in Latin America).

A significant characteristic of Guatemala is the fact that at least half of the population is Mayan, from some 21 distinct ethno-linguistic groups. Once again, poverty has caused a great deterioration in their living conditions, and 80 per cent of those living in poverty are indigenous people. In some regions, the population is mainly Mayan, for example in Quiché, Huehuetenango, and Las Verapaces (all high-risk zones). In these regions there is only one doctor for every 10,000 inhabitants, and the illiteracy rate is over 80 per cent. There is also a total absence of services like telephones, electricity, and safe drinking water.

The indigenous populations living in the identified risk zones, which coincide with the places where the majority of the displaced communities have resettled, are extremely vulnerable — the result of a long history of discrimination, exploitation, marginalisation, and exclusion. However, they have survived and held on to their identity in these conditions because of the quasi-democratic nature of their socio-religious structures and high levels of coherence in their communities, including a tradition of self-government and service to the community.

In Guatemala one of the most notable elements of female vulnerability is widowhood, largely due to the 30 years of conflict. One in ten women in the country is a widow, almost half a million women. Today it is officially estimated that more than 17 per cent of Guatemalan households are headed by women, although it is unofficially estimated that the true figure is much higher.

In terms of health, in addition to acute respiratory infections, illnesses caused by parasites, diarrhoea, and skin diseases which affect the whole of the population, Guatemalan women suffer alarming levels of anaemia, malnutrition, and serious complications during pregnancy. Most nursing women suffer from nutritional anaemia, and maternal mortality is conservatively estimated at 22 per 10,000 live births. In fact, nutritional deficiencies constitute the fourth-highest cause of female mortality. Although no official statistics were obtainable, it is generally agreed that the situation is even worse among rural and indigenous women.

Table 14: Vulnerability among Guatemalan women

Indicator	Value
Widows	9.2% of the female population (almost half a million)
Households headed by women	17% of households (under-recorded)
Illiteracy (women over 15)	48% of women (national average) 60% of rural women
Principal causes of female mortality (all ages)	1. Intestinal infections (18.4%) 2. Respiratory infections (17.5%) 3. Perinatal causes (15.3%) 4. Nutritional deficiencies (6.5%)
Maternal mortality	22 per 10,000 live births It is estimated that among indigenous women maternal mortality is 50% greater
Maternal malnutrition (mothers aged between 15 and 49)	33%
Anaemia	6 out of 10 nursing women suffer from nutritional anaemia

Sources: FLACSO, 1997; OPS/PAHO, 1993 and 1996; INE, 1995

The high-risk areas identified by the mapping are also zones of high vulnerability, particularly because most of the marginalised population is concentrated there. These are also areas where maternal malnutrition is significantly higher than the national average (see Table 15).

Table 15: Vulnerability among women in Guatemala (by region)

Indicator	Capital	Central	South-west	North	North-west, North-east, and Petén	Regional average
Maternal mortality (per 10,000 live births)	7.4	14.1	14.5	18.2	15.2	13.2
Maternal malnutrition	21%	27.8%	42.8%	43%	41%	35.1%

Sources: INE, 1995 and OPS, 1993

46

High levels of illiteracy, especially where there are marked differences between the sexes, restrict the access of women to resources. This helps to explain why, in an emergency situation, they remain at the margins when assistance is offered. Given the large distances between rural communities and health centres, their prospects are very poor.

El Salvador

El Salvador, with a population of 6 million living in 21,000 km² (an area roughly the size of Wales), is the most densely populated country in the region, with 270 inhabitants per km² and one-quarter of the population living in the capital city. Although 55 per cent of the people live in rural areas, barely 9 per cent of the GNP comes from agricultural production. In a context of rural deprivation, along with structural adjustment measures that aim to strengthen the service sector (business, banks, and tourism) and industry, the rural population survive through subsistence farming and monthly remittances from relatives in the USA. The aggregate income from these remittances, together with the cancellation of the debt to the USA (US$464m), has allowed the country to create the economic reserves necessary to counter the effects of recession and inflation, and explains El Salvador's economic 'stability' in the post-war period.

Levels of poverty are high: 75 per cent of the population is classified as poor, with extreme poverty at 52 per cent. The distribution of poverty reflects the pattern of the war, with the former conflict zones showing the greatest concentration. Poverty is particularly high in the rural areas, with 36 per cent of *campesino* farmers living in extreme poverty. In 1990, half of the 0.5m people dependent on the informal urban economy were women, of whom 70 per cent were earning just US$2 per day. Of the households living in extreme poverty, 36 per cent were headed by women and 52 per cent of such households were headed by an illiterate adult. In 1992, the adult illiteracy rate was 23 per cent and was five times as high in the rural areas as in the towns.

The principal causes of death from disease are intestinal infections, respiratory illnesses, and sickness caused by parasites. The infant mortality rate is 57.4 per 1,000 live births, though this rises to 73 in the areas affected by the war. The maternal mortality rate is one of the highest in the continent. The principal causes are haemorrhages and septicaemia (only 53 per cent of births take place in health centres), combined with maternal malnutrition. The fertility rate is high, at more than five children per woman, and female contraceptive use is low at 50 per cent.

Honduras

Honduras comes after Nicaragua in the UNDP Human Development Index, occupying 114th position, even though many of its social indicators have moderately improved. The GNP per capita is approaching US$600 a year, which is the equivalent of the GNP recorded in the 1970s. Although just over half of the 6.5m population live in rural areas, only 20 per cent of GNP comes from agricultural production, suggesting that most rural families live and work at subsistence level.

Marginalisation in Honduras does not run solely along socio-economic, urban/rural, or gender lines. There are also great geographical inequalities, meaning that almost all the communities in certain departments or regions are socially excluded; and the most marginalised areas are also those at greatest risk of natural disasters. The levels of poverty in Honduras are similar to those in other countries in the region, with 75 per cent of households classified as being on the poverty line, which corresponds to 64 per cent of urban households and 87 per cent of households in rural areas. However, in high-risk areas such as western and southern Honduras, nine households in ten are on the poverty line, according to the Department of Social Planning. They are also the areas with the highest levels of illiteracy, way above the national level of 32 per cent, reaching 46 per cent in western Honduras and 37 per cent in the south. Living conditions are similarly worse than average in these two areas. The levels of overcrowding, lack of access to drinking water, and lack of basic sanitation are 18 per cent, 53 per cent, and 56 per cent higher respectively than the national average. The national maternal death rate is 220 per 100,000 live births, and is likely to be higher still in these two areas of Honduras. Almost half of those living in the rural areas have no access to health care.

Nicaragua

Time and again Nicaragua has borne the brunt of the natural disasters that have occurred in the region over the last two decades. The Pacific region is a very high-risk area, because of the high probability of a combination of multiple threats occurring, including drought. The Atlantic region is also at high risk, principally because of its level of marginalisation, and the high probability of hurricanes and floods occurring.

Nicaragua has experienced the fastest rate of social and economic deterioration of all the Latin American countries in the last decade, and is now the second poorest in the hemisphere after Haiti. It fell to 117th position in the UNDP 1996 Human Development Index, and its GNP per capita (US$390) is the equivalent of that of the 1950s — in other words, it has fallen back by 50 years. While in the 1985 socio-demographic survey 64 per cent of households were below the poverty line, the 1993 figure had risen to 75 per cent, with those living in extreme poverty rising from 27 per cent to 40 per cent of the population. Some 60 per cent of urban households and 85 per cent of rural households are now classified as poor.

Nicaragua's cities are also growing at the fastest rate in Latin America, with 66 per cent of the population now living in urban areas. Fifty per cent of GNP comes from service industries, 20 per cent from manufacturing, and 30 per cent from agricultural production. However, unemployment stands at 21 per cent, and under-employment at 53 per cent. The decline in purchasing power even for those with salaries has been dramatic: a salary worth 100 units in 1980 is now equivalent to a salary of 14 units. The minimum wage covers less than one-third of staple goods (almost exclusively food).

Despite the reduction of illiteracy to 13 per cent during the period of revolutionary Sandinista rule in the 1980s, primary-school drop-out rates and the disuse of literacy skills have pushed national illiteracy levels back to 29 per cent or more. (The average rate in the Pacific region stands at 13 per cent, because of greater access to services, but the figure for the Atlantic coastal region is approaching 33 per cent.) However, Nicaragua is the only country in the region where women's levels of literacy and average schooling are equal to or even greater than those of men. This can be attributed to more than a decade of war, and also to the seasonal or permanent migration of men in search of work, factors which also explain the high proportion of households headed by women which, at 30 per cent nationwide, is the highest in the region.

The stabilisation and structural adjustment measures have had a negative impact on all Nicaraguans, in that public-spending cuts have particularly slashed services which provided for women's needs – services such as nurseries, rural

health centres, and meal centres for children (*comedores infantiles*). The reduction in the health budget has meant fewer health services and a rapid deterioration in the quality of those that remain, with the resulting consequences for basic health standards (Agurto 1997).

Table 16: Vulnerability among Nicaraguan women

Indicators	Value
Widows	8% of all women (183,683 women)
Households headed by women	28% of households
Illiteracy (age 10+)	24%
Causes of female mortality (all ages)*	1. Accidents 2. Circulatory illnesses 3. Perinatal Causes 4. Tumours
Causes of illness in women	1. Circulatory illnesses 2. Perinatal causes 3. Tumours (26% affecting the reproductive organs)
Maternal mortality	6.8% per 10,000 live births

Source: FLACSO, 1997
* not necessarily the primary causes of death

Nicaraguan women have a strong presence in the informal economic sector, and it is not unusual for it to be the woman who finances the purchase of seed for the annual harvest with money obtained from selling food, clothes, fruit, etc. This is because 43 per cent of rural women work principally in the business and service sectors, compared with 17 per cent of men. At the same time, 45 per cent of rural women work in agriculture, producing mainly sesame seed, potatoes, coffee, sugar cane, and vegetables, raising livestock and farming poultry; as many as three-quarters of rural women contribute to the raising of small livestock (FIDEG 1996).

The significant participation of women in the rural economy points to the importance of involving them to a similar degree in emergency programmes. Above all they need access to resources to make up for losses suffered in production, especially because their involvement in organisations is limited (see Table 17). On average only one in four women is involved in social organisations; of these, 58 per cent belong to savings and credit co-operatives. In the event of an emergency it would be necessary to identify viable channels for resources so that they benefit women and their families.

Table 17: Involvement of women in social organisations in Nicaragua

Involvement of women in social organisations in Nicaragua	% of total members	% in positions of leadership
Rural organisations	15.5%	No data
Farming co-operatives	14.3%	8.9%
Savings and credit co-ops	57.8%	35.9%
Industrial/artisanal co-ops	32.8%	26.1%
Fishing co-ops	9.2%	8.5%

Source: FIDEG 1996

Women on the Atlantic Coast of Nicaragua, a high-risk zone, experience greater levels of vulnerability than those on the Pacific Coast, for various reasons. Here they have even less involvement in community organisations, although the figure varies according to cultural and ethnic groups. In most cases, it is the men who manage the resources for the community, through organisations like communal commissions (*comisiones comunales*). This has important implications for emergency situations, because of the central role that such groups play: when disasters strike, the needs of women are often not identified by the commissions, and it is through them that resources are channelled. An exceptionally high proportion of households is headed by women: almost half of all households in Bonanza (a mining zone), for instance. In addition to these factors, the geographical marginalisation of the Atlantic Coast makes emergency response, prevention, and mitigation work more difficult.

The Pacific region of Nicaragua enjoys the lion's share of the country's infrastructure and services. It is also the most densely populated area of the country. However, the region also registers the greatest levels of rural poverty in the country, principally in the western area

(León and Chinandega), with 99 per cent of the population classified as poor. This same area bore the brunt of the crisis in the agricultural export sector, with the result that a significant proportion of people who were formerly agricultural wage-labourers now exists without any chance of employment and no land for subsistence. The rest of the rural population are *campesino* farmers, living on arid land with little agricultural potential. According to a 1997 UNICEF survey, the drought resulted in women resorting to cooking roots, banana skins, and *guasimo* seeds, all of which caused food poisoning, particularly among children. The greatest effects of natural disasters, such as the eruption of the Cerro Negro volcano, the 1992 tidal wave, and the recent drought, have also been concentrated in this same area.

The region's infant-mortality rate is lower than the national average, principally because it is better served by health centres (60 per cent of Nicaragua's health services are concentrated in Managua and the departmental capitals of this region). By contrast, the infant-mortality rate for the Atlantic Coast is 34 per cent higher than the national average, not only because of the level of poverty but also because of extremely limited access to health care. Childhood malnutrition is high (29 per cent) for Nicaragua as a whole, though far higher still among poor and extremely poor households. Significantly, a 1991 survey found that 71 per cent of salaried households had a calorie-deficient diet, and 55 per cent ate less protein than necessary (Agurto 1997). Despite the correlation between women-headed households and (extreme) poverty, food deficiencies were higher overall in households headed by men. This suggests that women are better than men at managing and distributing household resources, even when fewer resources are available.

In terms of housing, well over one-third of households on the Pacific Coast and almost half of those on the Atlantic Coast are over-crowded; many have earth floors and lack clean drinking water or basic sanitation. Such households are highly vulnerable to the threat of flooding and hurricanes, to which they are greatly exposed.

The combined impacts of the Cerro Negro eruption and the recent drought on the northern Pacific Coast merit special attention here, partly because of the effects on women and girls. The very high levels of maternal and infant malnutrition in the area, added to food shortages caused by the drought, make pregnant or nursing women highly vulnerable.

Many premature births are already caused by the mother's poor nutritional status, and health workers fear that this situation will become even more acute in the coming months, because of increasing food shortages. The effects of the drought go beyond basic grain production, extending to vegetable produce and affecting the raising of small livestock, which are the main productive activities involving women. Diseases and the burning of grazing land have killed the weeds, insects, worms, and other organisms on which hens and pigs feed, causing sickness and starvation in some animals. Where the animals have survived, women have been forced to sell them to buy maize, not only eliminating the alternative food sources so important for safeguarding the food security of the family, but also reducing the intake of calories and protein which these provide (eggs, milk, chicken), thus intensifying the impact of this disaster and their vulnerability to subsequent catastrophes. Water has also become scarce in the area, with wells of up to 190m in depth now dry or yielding only very contaminated and dirty water. Families are rationing the use of water to levels that are inadequate to maintain decent standards of hygiene as well as for drinking and cooking.

4 Assessment of local capacity

It is important, but it can be difficult, to assess existing capacity to respond to an emergency: firstly because there may not be access to information about the nature of the situation; and secondly because of the large number of factors to be taken into account.

This section is divided into three parts. The first looks at the institutional framework for managing disasters and tries to identify and assess the capacity of regional, national, and local actors in Mexico and Central America, especially those institutions established by law for this purpose. The second examines some of the relevant civil-society organisations. The third covers a selection of actors and initiatives which contribute to building capacity to respond to emergencies in the region, or which may start to include this in the future. We have not included here any details about local NGOs, except where these have a legally defined function, since this information is necessarily somewhat ephemeral and incomplete.

The institutional framework

The only regional institution to have made important contributions to providing management support for the reduction of natural disasters in Central America is CEPREDENAC. It supports its members by improving their capacity to monitor dangerous natural phenomena, particularly those related to earthquakes, volcanoes, and wet-weather systems. It also focuses on the mapping of threats and risks in the region. A new emphasis in its recent work has been to seek effective links between national processes and local management capacity.

This is clearly the most important and stable institution in the region, as much in the policy aspects as in its capacity to build relationships with a variety of regional and international organisations. Its weaknesses reflect the inability of some of the member countries to define their priorities in the field of disaster reduction, and to attract appropriate funding; and also the problems it faces in promoting disaster prevention, particularly in the political arena.

Since 1996, regional initiatives to improve gender-related responses to emergencies have been promoted under the co-ordination of CEPREDENAC, whose strategic plan includes ensuring a focus on gender in all its work, with the aim of promoting women's participation in the prevention and mitigation of disasters. One of the first tasks of its Gender Co-ordination Unit was to consult with women throughout the region who were involved in disaster-related work, and to establish new mechanisms for mutual learning and for participation. This consultation process led to the First Constructive Central American Meeting on 'Gender and Disaster Culture', held in November 1996. This produced the following action plan for 1997:

- To carry out a participative investigation into gender, in order to examine the involvement of Central American women in disaster-related work.

- To incorporate a gender focus in the activities developed by national and regional actors in disasters.

- To design and reproduce material for public dissemination on gender and disasters, specifically in relation to the socio-cultural conditions in each country.

- To hold a national workshop on gender and disasters, aimed at training staff from government institutions and NGOs involved in disasters; to undertake training activities in each country; to promote the inclusion of a gender focus in disaster training at national and regional levels.

- To set up an office for the Regional Gender Co-ordination Unit.

- To hold a second regional meeting on gender and disasters.

A proposal and budget have been prepared, but to date funds have not been forthcoming. However, the regional team still carries out some activities, which have included establishing women's groups focused on the theme of gender and disasters in all the Central

51

American countries, although not in Mexico. The groups consist mainly of women who specialise in disasters or gender and represent various civil organisations, but they also include representatives of various ministries in each country. The initiative is unusual: there are few if any other countries with a national women's group specifically focused on gender and disasters with such broad-based representation. This is an area that could be much strengthened by creative international co-operation.

At the national level the work is very varied, though there is a degree of homogeneity in the work related to the development of systems for the prevention and management of disasters. Two important issues emerge here. The first is the lack of organisations with a sufficiently broad vision of the reduction of risks and the consequences of disasters. The second is the strong presence and dominance of the Armed Forces in the organisations that manage disasters (with the exception of Costa Rica).

We offer a brief summary of the situation in each country, but give a more detailed account of the situation in Mexico, given the complex policy framework for disaster management.

Mexico

Following the devastating earthquakes of 19 and 20 September 1985 in Mexico City, the President created the National Commission for Reconstruction. The next year, the National System for Civil Protection (SINAPROC) was established by presidential decree. The system consists of a programme (prevention, assistance, and protection), advice (consultative organisations) and a body of volunteers at three levels of government (federal, state, and municipal). The structure integrates staff from the public administration; from the co-ordinating bodies among the federations; from the states and municipalities; and representatives of social movements which take part in protecting civilians. These make up the institutional co-ordination in the General Management of Civil Protection in the Government Secretariat (DGPC). A technical assessment unit exists alongside the National Centre for the Prevention of Disasters (CENAPRED).

The main work of this body is to attend to and assist the population in case of disaster. Thus, in disaster situations the response of the state and federal institutions (including the Armed Forces), as well as that of national and international NGOs, depends upon a formal request from the municipal, state, and federal authorities successively. This is important, since in theory each state or municipality should have the capacity and resources to respond to any type of disaster. However, depending on the magnitude of the event, there is the possibility that other larger organisations, including external ones, will intervene to offer assistance and support, provided that the immediate authorities publicly declare an emergency and formally request their intervention.

This decentralised approach is a sensitive and controversial issue, and it can be a matter of life and death for those at risk. This is because local politicians tend to refrain from declaring emergencies, in order to avoid the intervention of the federal bodies and the Armed Forces, which do not have a good record in this area.

In practice, the system has the capacity for monitoring and planning for emergencies (Civil Protection Programme 1995–2000) and the material resources to ensure an appropriate response, provided that the emergency is not on a huge scale. However, the major problem is ensuring the effectiveness of this capacity, given the lack of engagement with the populations at risk. Of course, not all municipal and state committees are active, and in some areas the population rarely takes part in the civil protection plans. In combination with the political polarisation, such factors are affecting the programme.

Further, the operational plans do not contain a focus on gender, to judge from the contingency plans for eruptions of Popocatépetl and from the response to Hurricane Pauline in 1997. Implementation is in the hands of SINAPROC, state governments, presidents and municipal delegates, public representatives, and all the technical and government bodies. Few women are included in these teams. Nor has the formation of working groups, emergency brigades, and volunteers taken into account the need to recruit women and encourage their participation.

The evacuation plans cover the whole population, but without giving priority to pregnant women, old people, and disabled people. Nor does the management of refuges and hostels take into account the security of unaccompanied girls and women, above all to ensure protection from the sexual harassment that often arises among large concentrated populations. To date, no adequate measures have been drawn up, such as special accommodation for vulnerable women, or the inclusion of female staff in the protection units.

The products stored in warehouses do not include items for preparing food. The experience with Hurricane Pauline illustrated this: a week after it struck, the government finally responded to the demands of women and organised donations of cooking utensils, a need that should be predicted in any emergency situation. The importance of distributing the food via the women was not considered, and it had not been recognised that a food-distribution system controlled by men flies in the face of traditional practice in which the women assume the main role in acquiring and preparing the food. Overall, the operational plans are not based on a consideration of gender, nor on the affected population's capacity or participation, but on the central plans designed in Mexico City, which are almost totally independent of the communities and their organisations. Essentially, the situation is no different in Guatemala and Nicaragua with regard to their respective government institutions.

Guatemala

The National Emergency Committee (CONE) was founded in 1969 in the wake of Hurricane Francelia and became a permanent body in 1971. In mid-1994 CONE submitted a draft bill for the establishment of the National System for the Reduction of Disasters (SINRED) (prevention, mitigation, preparedness, response, rehabilitation, and reconstruction), taking into account international agreements on the need for appropriate legislation for disasters. SINRED implements its programmes and action through the National Commission for the Reduction of Disasters (CONRED, the new designation for CONE), and each ministry is looking at forming a Unit for the Reduction of Disasters within its structure. The General Council is the management body of SINRED; it consists of five ministers, representatives from the corporate sector, urban-development advisers (Planning Secretariat), and media advisers. The approval of the law was a surprise to many civil-society organisations, because they were not consulted, and the regulations are being drawn up without their involvement.

Through the Social Prevention Department, CONRED aims to encourage various social sectors to train up in the prevention of natural disasters, and is beginning to prioritise the role of women. Thus, a workshop was held in October 1995 with leading women from eight departments, representatives of the National Women's Office, and 10 special guests from the capital, in the hope that their participation in the departmental organisation and decision making would encourage the participation of other women and men in society. In particular, the workshop took note of the increased visibility of and scope for Guatemalan women to participate in the reduction of disasters through various groups, and urged their inclusion in all levels of emergency organisations.

Among the proposals are capacity-building and awareness-raising for women on gender analysis, in order to encourage the active participation of women in the prevention of disasters and in setting up local emergency committees. However, women's participation is seen in quantitative rather than qualitative terms. Though increasing the numbers of women on such committees is clearly important, the analysis does not include an examination of the ways in which disasters affect women and men differently, nor of the particular needs of women in disaster situations, or the application of a gender perspective in emergency programmes (for example in distribution systems, the provision of water, and public-health measures).

El Salvador

The National Committee for Emergencies (COEN), established in September 1976, is a leading institution that brings together various relevant actors. Opinions differ with respect to the role of COEN. Some think that 'there is no lead organisation in disasters, and COEN continues to be essentially a political body which hinders any work undertaken by others, and reflects an outmoded view of the issues' (personal communication from staff of LA RED).

Various attempts have been made to create a national system, but none has achieved the desired results. The Italians, along with the Pan-American Health Organisation (PAHO), have played an important role in establishing the Inter-institutional Technical Committee (COTIDE) to facilitate the decentralisation of decision-making and to encourage wider participation in order to improve disaster prevention and mitigation capacity.

Honduras

The System for the Response to and Prevention of Disasters (SAPD) was established in March 1972 with the creation of the Permanent Council for National Emergencies (COPEN). It aimed to turn the Armed Forces into the axis or reference point for the public, and to extend the state apparatus (Romano 1996). In December 1990, COPEN was replaced by the Permanent Commission for Contingencies (COPECO). Currently COPECO is trying to set up a system of co-ordination and support at national, regional (military regions), departmental, and municipal levels, and to include community emergency committees.

COPECO's executive secretary is appointed by the President of the country, and the post is currently held by a high-ranking military officer. The state secretariats, the Central Bank, and representatives of some rural associations make up COPECO. However, the most important peasant organisation in the country, COCOH, is not invited to participate, while one that is more sympathetic to the government's policies has been asked to join.

Nicaragua

There has been no overall system for disaster prevention, mitigation, and response in Nicaragua. Rather, ordinary citizens have had to organise themselves. Successive governments over the last 25 years have created structures and laws that have survived somehow or another, but are not fully used.

In operational terms, it is the High Command of National Civil Defence (EMNDC) that is the permanent institution in charge of disaster management, through the National Committees for Emergencies, which lay down the policies. Its efforts are concentrated on creating municipal committees for prevention, mitigation, and response to disasters, and on forming civil-defence brigades.

There is a group of Nicaraguan women working on CEPREDENAC's gender and emergency programme, but its proposals have come to nothing, for lack of funds. It includes women from various organisations, including the Ministry of Education, the Nicaraguan Women's Institute (INIM), and NGOs such as the Augusto César Sandino Foundation (FACS) and the Companions of the Americas. Some of the activities include encouraging women's participation in the training in prevention that is carried out with students, teachers, education brigades, rescue teams, and others. They share the concern that the courses organised by EMNDC (with the support of OFDA, the US Office for Disaster Response) to train trainers in the management of disasters and the assessment of the damage and needs are almost totally aimed at men.

The women's organisation could play an important part in emergencies at the national and local levels, not only in preventive work but also in its own emergency programmes. INIM is, for example, developing sustainable vegetable gardens in response to the drought, with techniques that might be more widely applied, since they are low-cost, simple, and economical in their use of water, as well as enhancing food security. However, the group is well aware of its own need to learn more about gender and disasters: its current members tend to specialise either in emergencies or in gender, and there is a need to integrate the two areas, both in theory and in practice.

Costa Rica

The National Emergencies Commission (CNE) was established in August 1969 by executive decree. Its predecessor was the Civil Defence, which started work in 1965. The CNE has undergone various restructuring processes, and by 1994 it was an autonomous, specialised, and well-resourced institution which was accorded a high priority by the government. The CNE has since come under the Ministry of Works and Transport and is fighting to maintain the quality of its disaster management, despite constraints on its resources.

Regional overview

The various institutions in the region share a series of problems. SINAPROC in Mexico and COEN in El Salvador are dependent on their governments and operate through the equivalent of the Interior Ministry or Home Office. The CNE in Costa Rica depends on the President of the Republic and is attached to the Ministry for Works and Transport, while COPECO in Honduras, CONRED in Guatemala, and EMNDC in Nicaragua also depend on the President and on the operational wing of the Ministry of Defence.

The quality of management and response to emergencies is varied, but corresponds largely to the twin common denominators of poverty and low political priority, which translate into constraints on the human and material resources for running national emergency plans. Overall, the official institutions are more concerned with responding to the impact of a disaster than with prevention, mitigation, and preparedness. It is difficult to assess the quality and effectiveness of their responses, but public observations are incorporated in Table 18.

Table 18: National capacity for emergency response in the region

Conditions	Weaknesses	Opportunities
Lack of resources	Low prioritisation on the political agenda	Prevention, mitigation, and preparedness are included in some development policies
Frequent changes in the political arena	Lack of clear regional policies for prevention, mitigation and preparation	Initial interest in prevention and mitigation at the decision-making level
Unequal participation of countries in the regional processes of prevention, mitigation, and preparedness	Low level of participation of civil society in regional decisions	Priority for environmental management and ordnance surveys at regional level
Different and changing threats and vulnerabilities	Intervention not co-ordinated with international assistance	Interest in raising the social impact of regional projects to reduce disasters
Growing threats and vulnerabilities	Little exchange of experiences	Institution created specifically for the purpose (CEPREDENAC)

Other widespread perceptions are that emergency responses are generally delayed (usually not operational until 48 hours after the event); that emergency plans are not widely known and exist only on paper; that the national emergency committees are closed institutions which do not allow civil society to participate, and when they do they invite only their political sympathisers; that emergency interventions reflect political interests, and rehabilitation and reconstruction programmes are exploited for electoral and propaganda purposes; that responses favour groups located in accessible places; and that aid distribution often favours friends and acquaintances, rather than reaching the people most in need.

The formal bodies are weak for several reasons. They lack qualified staff, and do not always enjoy the necessary financial and political support. They tend to take a narrow view of the problems caused by natural disasters and how to reduce them, and to look at these in sectoral or specialised terms, rather than taking a global approach. They lack the capacity to identify solutions and priorities in risk reduction, which in turn means that they are unable to formulate coherent and fundable projects. And finally, few of them co-ordinate adequately (or at all) with local institutions in order to respond effectively to emergency situations. Overall, then, the responsive capacity at the national level is generally weak, and is worsened by the lack of co-ordination and the reliance on improvised plans. All of this further complicates the situation of the affected populations.

It is at the local level where projects to reduce risks appear to have the most chance of producing concrete results. This is mainly due to the fact that many such projects are run by international organisations (although in collaboration with national and local structures) whose abilities are recognised (such as PAHO, the Red Cross, and the Organisation of American States). However, this tends to obscure the lack of national capacity to work at the local level. Further, local-level capacity is very weak, despite the priority that the international agencies have given it, and is totally inadequate to meet the needs of the many communities living in high-risk conditions.

Let us take the example of Mexico, where work at the state and municipal levels should have been a high priority, given the decentralised SINAPROC model, and the magnitude of the risks. Around Popocatépetl are more than 200 communities who belong to various states and municipalities who, according to SINAPROC, have received training in how to respond to emergencies. A field visit proved that these local capacities did not exist. Firstly, the system to warn of volcanic eruptions is not clear to the public: the system of signals (which uses the traffic-light colours) to indicate the level of alert is not fully understood by the local authorities or by the public, and there is confusion over whether or not the red alert is a signal to proceed with evacuation. It is unclear what local resources are available to mobilise people, and their supply is in any case highly dependent on external support. No local mapping has been done, let alone a realistic survey of the actual composition of the population and its needs. Instead, calculations are based on the last census, which is out of date. Secondly, the local resources are scarce. In Tlamanalco, for example, there is not even one ambulance, and the mayor is having problems finding fuel for the police and to run the municipality. Thirdly, despite SINAPROC's incompetence, there are no other organisations that might help to build up local capacities.

In El Salvador, COEN and the Salvadoran Red Cross have tried to build up capacities at the municipal level to cope with emergency situations, although UNDP claims that only 16 municipalities out of a total of 262 have the minimum capacity to respond.

In Nicaragua, EMNDC, in collaboration with public and private institutions, has achieved some success in setting up Municipal Committees for Prevention, Mitigation and Response to Disasters, in training, in organising civil-defence brigades (First Aid, Fire Service, Rubble Clearance, Search and Rescue), drawing up risk maps, and drafting disaster-management guidelines. However, they have had some success only in 22 of the 131 municipalities in the country, of which 57 have been declared as 'high priority'.

In Costa Rica, the CNE has prioritised 112 communities situated in approximately 70 regions, and has organised local emergency committees in 90 per cent of these. However, training has been very limited.

The situation is particularly difficult in Guatemala. For instance, the San Roque community in the south of the country comprises about 100 families who survive on locally grown maize and sesame. However, the River Ocosito often overflows and floods the cultivated fields. The community is unclear about the level of risk that the river poses to them and their crops, and no organisation has offered even basic training in responding to emergencies. This is not an isolated case. CONRED argues that resource constraints mean that is impossible to meet all the needs of communities at high risk.

In general, some local-level capacity-building is taking place, either via the official government institutions or through the intervention of specialised international organisations developing pilot projects. But this is a very slow process in comparison with the rate at which the threats are increasing. Underlying problems such as the lack of human and material resources, the poor regional–national–local links, and the politicisation of disasters are not readily overcome. Local actions allow for an understanding of the problems at the grassroots level. The strengthening of local organisations gives a genuine impetus to self-management and is a step towards real operational capacity. Eventually, this could help to increase the pressure on other actors, particularly in the political arena.

Thus, although it is important to support local-level initiatives, the wider context should not be ignored, and neither should the need for decentralised planning and for co-ordinated action. This is where policies for prevention and not only for preparedness can best be promoted. The risk of concentrating only on the local level is that this could ultimately lead to a lack of efficient co-ordination.

Disasters and civil society

Formally, disaster management in Mexico and Central America appears to be the exclusive domain of the governments. Few civil-society organisations, in particular NGOs, are present in this area and enjoy recognition for their work. Although many organisations work on development and/or the environment, they seldom include emergency work in their programmes.

One reason for this may be the recent direction and priorities of international assistance; another may be the problem of harmonising these areas of work in such a complex situation, where many such organisations focus on the struggle against poverty and the increase of socio-economic conflicts. Whatever the explanation, the reality is that there is a notable lack of involvement in these areas, an absence that is worrying, given the concentration of highly vulnerable populations in areas of high risk, and where government assistance has often been less than effective. Civil-society organisations perhaps need to adopt a two-pronged strategy for emergency and development, given their considerable organisational potential and the knowledge drawn from their experience of working with grassroots communities.

Certain civil-society actors and initiatives represent an important body of knowledge that could be used in future emergency interventions. It also needs to be recognised that many organisations (such as trade unions, social movements, and NGOs) do not have an institutional mandate to work in emergency situations, but nevertheless offer support to members, partners, or affiliates who have suffered disasters. This has enabled them to 'learn by doing' and makes them potential counterparts for emergency work and candidates for training programmes.

There are also many international NGOs in the region with a recognised competency in emergencies and disasters (Catholic Relief Services, Médecins Sans Frontières, CARE, and Médecins du Monde, among others), but the majority work in other aspects of development. In situations of crisis, many of them do collaborate with the affected populations, if they are already among their own priority groups. However, we would emphasise the need for national and local NGOs to be involved in co-ordinating various aspects of emergency-related work.

One critical aspect here is the application of gender-fair policies in emergencies. Overall, there is very little knowledge of these matters either in the official emergency bodies, which are mainly technico-military teams with limited women's participation, or among NGOs. However, many NGOs do have some knowledge of gender and development, which is something on which to build.

Mexico

Despite Mexico's status as the country at the highest risk in the region, with the largest vulnerable and exposed populations, the weak participation of NGOs in Mexico in this field is remarkable by comparison with the rest of the region. However, NGOs do have a proven lobbying capacity, with networks such as *Convergencia* (convergence), *Seguridad Alimentaria* (Food Security), and *Combate contra la Pobreza* (Fight Against Poverty) having the potential to mobilise activity around the response to the hardships suffered by fellow citizens as a result of disasters.

In the southern region, particularly in Chiapas, civil-society organisations have demonstrated the capacity to focus their lobbying on measures to defuse the prevailing conflict. However, the capacity to respond actively to the populations affected by the conflicts is limited, especially when it is a question of displaced populations and those who have been forcibly evicted, where there are no clear intervention strategies.

Guatemala

There are organisations, such as the National Co-ordination Body for Indigenous and Rural Women (CONIC), which represent the interests of the most marginalised social sectors and which have shown some limited capacity to respond to emergencies, especially in areas where the government body has been ineffectual. Some niche organisations, such as the Guatemalan Association for Emergencies (AGE), focus on emergency-related work within a particular geographical area, while others, such as Friends of the Americas (a programme promoted by the US government through OFDA), are concerned with improving the security of schools throughout Central America.

The long politico-military conflict in Guatemala also gave rise to a large number of organisations and groups that defend human rights. As elsewhere in Latin America, these have a high number of female members. Their leaders and active members were themselves victims of persecution, disappearance, detention, and torture by the military and death squads. Women's solidarity-based organisations that have their historical roots in the conflict still play an important role in responding to the material, economic, political, and psycho-social needs of women, particularly widows and other women who have lost male family members, in the context of the reconstruction process. Organisations such as the Consultative Assembly of Displaced Populations focus on the obligations under the Peace Accords 'to put special emphasis on the protection of female headed households as well as widows and orphans which have been the most affected'. In addition, the returnee women's organisations which were initially formed during exile in Mexico, where they helped to promote the human rights and political, economic, and social development of the refugees, have remained active in Guatemala, although many women have succumbed to the pressure on them to return to their pre-war roles. These are also committed to ensuring the recognition and fulfilment of the agreements concerning displaced women, and to securing adequate economic resources for reconstruction. In many cases, they have helped to build solidarity between returnees, former displaced populations, and those who remained in Guatemala throughout the war. (The latter two groups did not benefit as the refugees did from international support.)

El Salvador

The Centre for Disaster Protection (CEPRODE) aims to 'design, implement and evaluate community protection programmes for the population in case of disasters and to conserve and restore natural resources in areas at high risk of natural disasters'. It also produces information and scientific studies on natural disasters and the environment; and encourages the protection of natural resources through research and joint projects with other institutions. CEPRODE has a strong influence and is well known in official circles and within civil society, and is linked to the regional processes in disasters and emergency work through the RED network. Its focus on action-research brings it into contact with local communities, in a line of work that the German technical assistance agency GTZ and ECHO of the European Commission are now pursuing.

The Lempa Foundation (FUNDALEMPA) is also carrying out key work in the area of disaster prevention through a proposal to produce detailed surveys (one of the few organisations in Central America which has this focus) of the Lempa river basin. It is developing an information system on the use of water (a critical resource in El Salvador) and the problems of flooding. The system relies on systematic monitoring of the disasters caused by floods: information that will form part of the Geographic Information System that is being set up. It is also looking for the most appropriate means to communicate this information to the communities at high risk.

Honduras

The Centre for Research and Control of Pollutants (CESCO) aims to control and also reduce pollutants and waste products, and to minimise their environmental effects. This area of work is critical in connection with disasters caused by human action.

Nicaragua

The Augusto César Sandino Foundation (FACS) has an emergency programme which has played a key role in the development of its capacity in matters concerning assessments, collection, and management of information, training for high-risk communities, and emergency response. It is arguably the only one in Nicaragua that is set up to put into practice the concept of developing capacity as part of a response to an emergency. FACS has extensive national and international influence in combining development, advocacy, and emergencies. For this reason, it is involved in co-ordinating and handling aid to those affected by disasters such as the 1992 tidal wave and Hurricane Joan in 1988. The current director of FACS belongs to the gender and disasters group, and the organisation is committed to involving women as well as men in the training programme, and being sensitive to the needs of widows and single women.

There are numerous other bodies in Nicaragua working on the Atlantic Coast that either are, or could become involved in, emergency work. Similarly, Costa Rica has a number of organisations with some capacity to undertake emergency work, or which are concerned with environmental issues.

Relevant actors and initiatives in the region

In this section, we offer a small illustrative sample of the wide variety of initiatives to reduce the scale and impact of disasters.

CEPREDENAC: The Co-ordinating Centre for the Prevention of Natural Disasters in Central America (CEPREDENAC) is a relatively young institution (part of SICA, a body that was established by the various Ministers of Foreign Affairs). CEPREDENAC is based in Panama and has already achieved regional and international recognition. It seeks to provide regional co-ordination for national initiatives in the context of natural disasters. It mainly links the monitoring work carried out by similar institutions with the emergency committees and with other important actors such as universities and other institutions which play an important part in prevention, mitigation, and preparedness. It acts as a broker or channel for funding for specific programmes, though it is not itself operational.

International Decade for the Reduction of Natural Disasters (IDRND) 1990–2000: With its headquarters in Costa Rica, the IDRND has encouraged activities aimed at reducing the number of disasters in the region. It focuses on information and is co-ordinating a project to create a Regional Centre for Information on Disasters (CRID), which will combine the efforts of PAHO/WHO, IFRCS, MSF, and the CNE in Costa Rica and also CEPREDENAC.

Pan-American Health Organisation (PAHO/WHO): PAHO is one of the pioneering organisations in health-related work on natural disasters and also provides technical health assistance. It is currently working on a project to provide university-level training on disaster preparedness in Central America to support the Central American Commission for Disasters, and on an Internet project to ensure better communication among the organisations involved in risk- management.

International Federation of Red Cross/Red Crescent Societies (IFRCS): As part of the Red Cross movement, the Federation brings together all the national Red Cross and Red Crescent Societies worldwide. At an international level, the International Committee of the Red Cross (ICRC) is charged with working in situations of armed conflict, and the Federation with responses to natural disasters and development, although the National Societies do not make this distinction. The Federation is currently working on strengthening the National Societies, training staff, and setting up its own communication system, both between the National Societies and within each country. Since 1995, it has been supporting community-level disaster-preparedness work in Guatemala, Nicaragua and Panama, with plans to extend to Costa Rica, El Salvador, and Honduras.

Organisation of American States (OAS): The OAS has undertaken a lot of disaster-reduction work in Mexico and Central America and has experience ranging from local work to region-wide initiatives. For example, the Programme for the Reduction of Vulnerability in the Education Sector to Natural Hazards promotes the development and implementation of policies, plans, projects, and preparedness for the reduction of natural disasters, focusing on physical infrastructure. The activities include technical assistance, training, and the transfer of technology. Pilot projects began in El Salvador and Nicaragua and have since 1995 extended to Costa Rica, Guatemala, Honduras, and Panama.

The Project for the Reduction of the Vulnerability of the Road Transport System in Natural Disasters in Central America and Andean countries is being conducted in collaboration with the Pan-American Institute for Roads, also with financial support from ECHO. It maps risks and local warning systems in Central America and is based on the pilot developed in Honduras. The Project for the Reduction of the Vulnerability of Small Urban Centres and the Pan-American Highway to Natural Disasters in Central America usefully integrates work on communication routes, people living in slums, and commercial activities with an assessment of the risks.

UNDP: The UNDP supports governments in various ways and also provides funds for responses to emergency situations. For instance, a project entitled Training and Strengthening for the Prevention and Management of Natural Disasters in Costa Rica seeks to support the CNE in strengthening municipal and local committees in their struggle against natural disasters. The Training for the Prevention of Natural Disasters Project in Nicaragua supports the training of local committees undertaken by EMNDC, while the Project for Support to the National Strategy for Environmental Education in El Salvador links environmental problems and natural disasters.

The Network of Social Studies for the Prevention of Natural Disasters in Latin America (LA RED): This is a network of institutions and researchers working in the field of disaster vulnerability from a social perspective. Costa Rica, Honduras, El Salvador and Guatemala belong to it, and its regional headquarters are based in the FLACSO office in Costa Rica.

Since 1994, LA RED has been implementing a programme of research and information exchange, geared to strengthening the local and regional capacity of organisations that work in disaster reduction (partly funded by ECHO). This programme also serves to disseminate relevant concepts, and to inform and influence the policies of the national governments and of regional and international organisations. While LA RED is not operational, many of its members are organisations that use the information in their work.

Other initiatives include **Médecins Sans Frontières** (MSF), whose regional office in Costa Rica plans to draw up an 'Emergency Preparedness Plan', and has sought to combine development and emergency project-management skills. The Economic Research Institute at the **University of Costa Rica** is embarking on a study of the economic consequences of natural disasters in the region. And finally, **Urgent Action International**, a French NGO, offers training in rehabilitation, as well as raising public awareness. It may also set up a logistics base to store goods and equipment to respond to future crises.

In terms of bilateral support in this field, the most active country appears to be Sweden, followed by Denmark, France, the UK, and the Netherlands. Germany is also starting to support work this area. Sweden has been a driving force in Central America in risk reduction. In 1988, Swedish funds enabled CEPREDENAC to set up as a research organisation, and this support has continued since CEPREDENAC re-defined its mission in 1993 as an initiative of SICA (System for Central American Integration). Since then, the Swedish Agency for Institutional Development (SIDA) has also funded national projects and the institutional strengthening of CEPREDENAC.

Denmark, in collaboration with CEPREDENAC, is particularly involved in the reduction of the risk of flooding in Central America, especially with a programme which aims to improve early-warning systems. France has mainly provided one-off support in the area of information about natural phenomena and preventive information, for example scientific projects like the research on volcanoes in Costa Rica.

Like the UK, the Netherlands has been weak in the areas of preparedness and prevention, but is currently supporting a project to reduce disasters in Costa Rica, under the UNESCO framework. This project aims to strengthen the scientific capacity to integrate knowledge about natural phenomena in order to produce a map on various scales (from 1/25,000) for planners.

While Germany has had little involvement in Central America (mainly supporting rural development projects or training programmes and small business development), its FEMID (Strengthening of Local Structures in Disaster Mitigation) project does aim to strengthen local structures by supporting research, training workshops, and small complementary projects in disaster reduction. The three-year project concentrates on a pilot area in each Central American country and will eventually move to exchanges between pilot areas to evaluate and compare the strategies and tools being used.

Italy has helped to set up a warning system in the areas threatened by the Cerro Negro, while Switzerland supports projects in Nicaragua and Guatemala related to the improvement of the network to monitor volcanoes and to improve early-warning systems for tidal waves. Finally, NORAD of Norway works with CEPREDENAC on a project to reduce the risk of earthquake damage in Central America. This project should result in a regional centre for information on earthquakes and the strengthening of the scientific and technical work of the various seismology institutes in their work.

5 Progress and needs in disaster management

Prevention and mitigation

Activities in this area are very much limited to the regional level, since few of the phenomena that occur in the region (mostly natural) can be prevented, while the more 'passive' tasks of prevention and mitigation are extremely costly.

Land planning

Effective planning in land-use is the basis for all policies of risk and disaster prevention. This is a highly sensitive issue, and yet the lack of adequate policies in the region increases with every disaster. The poorest communities are obliged to use high-risk land, as is increasingly apparent in every country. For example, in Guatemala, in the metropolitan area, there are more than 50 poor neighbourhoods or settlements situated on unstable slopes that are frequently affected by landslides, whether because of intense rains or because of seismic activity. Equally, there are other risks associated with the inappropriate housing of repatriated refugees, demobilised fighters, and returnees (with the situation of the Ixcán being the most egregious example). These communities are placed in the most unstable parts of the country, and without swift and appropriate intervention they will soon become 'environmental refugees'.

In Honduras, of 200 *barrios* or neighbourhoods that are classified as marginalised in the capital, Tegucigalpa, 80 are at high risk, mainly because they are so exposed. In San Salvador and its environs, the marginal *barrios* are devastated each year by the River Acelhuate, because they are so close to the river banks. The same thing happens in Nicaragua and Costa Rica. In practice, this highly irrational use of land is becoming the main risk factor for the population.

A strategy on Land Planning produced by the Central American Alliance for Sustainable Development (ALIDES) is possibly the most coherent and global in the region, but very few of its recommendations have been put into practice. At a national level, some efforts have been made, mainly in Costa Rica, where CNE produced a manual in 1993 on building in areas of natural threats. This is an attempt to educate the municipal and technical authorities on how to make the best use of land. However, little has changed. The great challenge is how to develop and implement a strategy to combat poverty, at the same time as taking into account the risk and disaster factors.

Causes of dangerous phenomena

Until now little could be done to intervene directly in dangerous events before they set off a chain of disastrous consequences. As we have seen, the main phenomena in the region are landslides, floods, and, to a lesser extent, drought. However, these cannot be separated from problems that have been caused by human agency, such as deforestation, which makes any intervention very complex. Reforestation projects, alternative farming, and forestry conservation are generally not linked to risk reduction: hence, despite some interesting initiatives by the EU and the World Bank, among others, the lack of progress in the region.

Civil protection projects and building regulations

Important steps have been identified in the area of public works, for example for flood protection, and there exist codes and laws for high-rise buildings in high-risk zones (liable to seismic activity and hurricanes). However, the economic situation and the lack of political will mean that the small constructions of this kind that have been built to date make an insignificant contribution to resolving the problems of floods in many parts of the geographical area. In addition, the design of these buildings often does not relate to the phenomena likely to be experienced. Some are even hazardous to the population themselves. For example, the dyke built to protect Cartago (Costa Rica) from the flow of sludge caused by the eruption of the Irazú in 1963 was dismantled because of structural weaknesses. In Nicaragua mini-dams built in the southern basin of Lake Managua to prevent flooding in the capital eventually became a risk-factor for the population living in the lower part of the basin. The public works that are really needed are very costly to build, which is partly why they are uncommon.

However, there have been certain initiatives to establish building regulations, though these tend to be observed only in public buildings and not in individual housing, which is precisely what is most vulnerable in the region. Most of these regulations are also inappropriate in the absence of proper seismic research in that area. Such studies have seldom been completed. For example, in Mexico there exists one study for the Estado de Colima, and now one is being considered for the capital; in El Salvador a study was recently completed with the support of UNAM for the area of San Salvador; in Nicaragua and Costa Rica, partial studies are being carried out for high-priority areas in Managua and San José respectively.

Table 19: Building codes for high-risk areas

Country	Codes and regulations
Mexico	Various (elaborated for each federal organisation)
Guatemala	Seismic Regulations for Guatemala City (1971) and Seismic Code Proposal (1979)
El Salvador	Regulation for Seismic Design (1996) and Technical Design Regulations (1994)
Honduras	None
Nicaragua	Seismic Code for Buildings in the Area of DN (1973) and Building Regulation (1983)
Costa Rica	Seismic Code (1986)
Panama	Design Regulation (1984)

Preparedness

The main objective of disaster-preparedness work is to tackle unavoidable events with the minimum of repercussions. This involves helping to build the capacity of communities at risk, and working with relief and response groups to enable them to confront crises, before, during, and after impact. These activities are increasingly organised in the region and are the essence of risk-reduction work.

Warning systems

Important advances have been in the warning systems for cyclone risk and, to a lesser extent, flood warnings (whether or not linked to tropical cyclones). Progress has also been made in hurricane warning systems, particularly in tracking them and forecasting their path, intensity, and speed.

This work forms part of the global system of meteorological vigilance that is managed by the World Meteorological Organisation (WMO), of which Central America and Mexico form the IV Regional Association. This system combines land, maritime, aerial, and satellite observation through Specialised Meteorological Centres, from where the information is distributed to countries by special high-velocity telecommuni-cations systems. Central American countries currently receive material processed in the US Regional Centre in Miami, and have adopted the improved Start-4 system.

The challenge is how to communicate the risk of a particular phenomenon to the population at large. This is where many problems arise, from interpretation on the one hand to the lack of any effective means of communicating with the population, especially in rural areas, on the other. There is also the problem of making the decision to issue a warning, which is often a highly centralised and politicised process. As a result, warnings may be given too late.

Flood-warning systems are underdeveloped, despite flooding being the most common natural phenomenon in the region. One difficulty is that it has not been possible to establish the level of risk, due to the lack of studies of the hydrological cycles and the hydrographic basins whose rivers are most likely to flood at any given time. All the Central American countries have been supported by the Nordic countries to install numerical systems of hydrological prediction, though unfortunately using models that have proved impractical. However, some specific pilot projects underway in El Salvador, Honduras, and Nicaragua may make it possible to widen the warning systems in the area, with Costa Rica being the most advanced.

It is important to note that the various mathematical models for predicting floods do not respond to the practical needs of the region. They are often adopted in order to keep up bilateral aid relationships, but their usefulness is limited to the institutions involved, and does not benefit the population which is threatened or at risk.

Preparation for protection

When dealing with a foreseen phenomenon, it is possible to take preventive measures, such as evacuating the population or setting up supply lines. When disaster actually strikes, people take their own steps to protect themselves.

Pre-emptive population evacuation is rarely carried out. A dreadful example of this inaction was seen during the eruption of the Chichonal volcano in Chiapas in 1982. Local people were practically forced to remain in their homes by the state authorities, with the tragic result that most of the Zoque indian population was buried by burning lava and volcanic ash. In Nicaragua, the people living around Bluefields on the Atlantic Coast were not evacuated during Hurricane César in 1996, even when it was known that it was about to strike. There are many similar examples in the region.

All of the disaster-related bodies in the region, official and non-governmental alike, produce information on what to do in the case of an earthquake, a flood, a fire, and so on. There are masses of material available. In Mexico, for instance, there is even a manual outlining a Family Protection Plan for Disasters. All this material is very useful, but it is not reaching the population at risk in an organised way. Rather, it frequently arrives in a muddled and incomplete form.

Preparation for relief

Relief organisations face a series of difficulties, especially with regard to the management of relief, which comes mainly from outside after the country has done what it can. Meanwhile, urgent needs are not covered during the first few hours after impact. Examples of this are the earthquake in Limon (Costa Rica), where more than 48 hours went by without urgent needs being attended to, the case of Hurricane César in Tasba Pauni (Nicaragua), and the fate of Francisco Léon (Mexico) with the eruption of Chichonal. Other serious problems lie in the poor co-ordination between relief organisations, and the frequent absence of immediately usable supplies such as medicine and food. And last but not least, the problem of communication, since there are seldom any means of communicating with affected areas. (Here, the network of radio enthusiasts in the region plays a significant role.)

In the relief phase, the Red Cross plays a very important role in each country. The extent of its work varies from one place to another, but it has made great efforts to respond in appropriate ways. The Mexican Red Cross is the best-equipped organisation, with many vehicles and a sophisticated global, regional, and national communications system.

Supply Management (SUMA) software has been employed by PAHO since 1991. Funded by the Netherlands, this software facilitates the administration of all kinds of supplies coming in from outside the catastrophe zone itself. PAHO has conducted extensive training in how to use the system, though several countries lack the equipment to make best use of it.

Emergency plans

Emergency plans have been formulated by the competent authorities in each country. They should encompass both national and local needs, depending on the risks and vulnerabilities identified. However these plans are not always comprehensive, especially in terms of risk. It is also questionable how effective they really are, since most of them are not up-to-date (though El Salvador and Guatemala have recently updated theirs, and Nicaragua is in the process of doing so). Often, they were produced to respond to immediate situations and, once these have passed, they become no more than reference material and are of no operational use in other situations. And although the region now faces frequent drought, it is noteworthy that the relevant ministries (Agriculture and Livestock) have no contingency plans for this challenge.

Other important factors regarding these national emergency plans have been identified by CEPREDENAC. For instance, only in Costa Rica and Guatemala is it a legal obligation to develop and follow emergency plans, and only Costa Rica has made its national emergency plan official. Furthermore, only in Costa Rica and El Salvador are the plans truly national in their coverage; in the other countries, they are only partial. Finally, not one of the plans is public knowledge within the country. In Honduras, the emergency plan is actually confidential.

63

There are very few NGOs with emergency plans, with the Red Cross being a notable exception. In Costa Rica, 16 organisations are developing a co-ordinated plan for technology-related emergencies and are preparing proposed legislation so that it can be officially recognised. PAHO supports the development of emergency plans at a regional level in the health sector and has its own Emergency Programme, as do the MSF offices.

Information and training

Awareness raising, training, and development play an important role in the work of reducing risk and vulnerability, and in disaster mitigation; and information is critical both in terms of advising people of the likely risks they face, and in sharing ideas about preventive steps that might be taken. In the region, information and training on response to natural catastrophes, and to a lesser degree to disasters of human agency, are produced mainly to support preparation for disasters.

Most of the work going on in this area is concerned with the dissemination of information on the threats, and to a lesser extent with how to prepare for the resulting emergencies. However, there is very little done in terms of prevention, apart from new programmes in Costa Rica and Mexico. In both cases, however, these are primarily concentrating on the development and application of earthquake-resistant engineering.

Prevention work relates to decisions taken at the highest level, which are shaped by political or funding considerations, and civil-society organisations are generally not involved. But in practice, the concept of prevention has scarcely been developed at all, especially among political actors.

The production and dissemination of information on natural disasters is achieved mainly through conferences, seminars, and workshops; specialised journals and websites; and documentation centres. The information is very diverse, ranging from detailed accounts of major events, to technical and social perspectives on disasters, to micro-studies such as the study of vulnerability of hospitals in Costa Rica. Some of the most widely circulated publications and well-used websites in the region include 'STOP Disasters' and the reports prepared by the IDRND; 'CEPREDENAC News', which is sent to members by email; and

Red Cross and PAHO publications, including the Red Cross compendium for natural-disaster management ('Series 3000'), among many others. (Once the international decade finishes, it is not clear whether the IDRND magazine will have the funding to survive.)

There is a considerable amount of information available on the Internet on the activities organised by official organisations in the field of natural disasters. CENAPRED in Mexico issues daily updates on 'Popo', and organisations such as the CNE (www.cne.go.cr) and the Regional Centre of Information on Disasters (www.netsalud.sa.cr/ops/crid) are useful sources. PAHO organised a Latin American Seminar for the Managing Information on Disasters on the Internet in late 1997.

Documentation centres are also valuable but, with the exception of the PAHO centre in Costa Rica, most have incomplete or very specialised holdings. PAHO's Disaster Documentation Centre (DDC) was set up to disseminate material to public as well as private organisations and to concerned individuals. Demands on the Centre are currently outstripping its capacity to respond, and moves are underway to link it with other libraries through a Regional System of Information on the Reduction of Natural Catastrophes, in order to expand its impact and reach in a more efficient way. Another initiative is the idea of converting the existing DDC into a Regional Centre for Information on Disasters as a multi-agency centre. PAHO, WHO, IDRND, CEPREDENAC, IFRCS, and MSF are in favour of this move.

However, the local communities, which ought to be the main recipients of information and training, are not being reached. Although this is a widely known problem and concern, nowhere did we find a properly structured programme for communicating information to the people at most serious risk. The Red Cross is a key actor in this area. By the very nature of its work, it is an organisation that works closely with communities and also has relatively good geographical coverage (though this is very patchy in some areas) and a wide scope of activities. For example, the Honduran Red Cross (established in 1937) is organising community-level disaster training workshops but is also participating in latrine-construction programmes with a view to reducing vulnerability in the most marginalised communities. It should also be pointed out that the majority of evacuation drills that take place in schools and other public and private buildings in the region are co-ordinated by the Red Cross, which is very involved in this kind of activity.

The Salvadoran Red Cross has a community training programme (part of the Series 3000) and organises disaster-preparedness courses on request. Workshops and training programmes are also being developed in Nicaragua, Costa Rica, and Panama, looking at local risks and trying to deal with the expressed needs of the communities.

There are a number of other initiatives, including those being sponsored or run by international agencies such as GTZ, or by multilateral agencies such as UNDP. Many NGOs also work in health and agricultural programmes and others connected with potential disasters, but this is seldom their main focus.

Overall, while there is very rich empirical knowledge of potential risks, based on on-the-ground experience, this has not been sufficiently exploited or valued, and much of the information and expertise is lost. There is little co-ordination of effort, and a general lack of communication and exchange among community leaders, trainers, and local groups on issues of natural disasters. The only positive example found in the mapping exercise was in Mexico, where, with the support of the World Council of Churches, a group of people affected by the Cerro Negro in Nicaragua and other victims of disasters in El Salvador visited communities threatened by Popocatépetl, where they shared their experiences and the lessons they had learned. It would be interesting, for example, if local committees and civil-society organisations in the region had the opportunity to share experience of the People's Local Emergency Committee (Comité Popular Local de Emergencia) of Limón (Costa Rica), which because of the lack of response from the competent authorities took responsibility for handling the emergency arising from the earthquake that destroyed the city on in April 1991.

Commendable efforts have been made in the region for informing specific social groups, but little has been done to raise awareness in certain key sectors, important in terms of prevention and preparation for emergency situations.

- **The education system:** more needs to be done to introduce the subject of disasters and their prevention into the school curriculum. Costa Rica, El Salvador, and Honduras have had some success in this area. Their Ministers of Education have created a special unit for this issue, and co-ordinate with other institutions, especially the National Emergency Committees and the Red Cross. On the other hand, universities and other training centres do not generally include this subject in their programmes, with a few notable exceptions. For example, at the faculty of law at the University of El Salvador, humanitarianism is included as part of the course on international law, and the engineering degrees in Costa Rica, Mexico, and Nicaragua cover earthquake-resistant structures. CENAPRED and the UNAM are also now running courses on the Global Administration of Disasters.

- **The media:** great efforts have been made to maintain a high level of information through the mass media. These are important channels for passing on knowledge and appropriate information to the public, to enable people to take better preventive action. Generally there is communication between the media and organisations responsible for disaster management.

- **Politics:** aspects of risk reduction and disaster mitigation can be developed without huge political commitment, especially with regard to disaster preparedness. This is not so for prevention, partly because of the high costs entailed and the very low level of awareness on the subject, but also because the technical specialists present convincing and persuasive arguments to the politicians. The key is to demonstrate to the politicians the cost-effectiveness of prevention, compared with reacting to the consequences of catastrophes. This situation partly explains why the competent authorities are often accorded only a low priority and have serious difficulties in keeping going. None has adequate funding for emergencies, or the necessary resources for their work to be truly efficient. However, and more positively, the establishment of the Central American Alliance for Sustainable Development (ALIDES) is a sign that certain issues are rising up the political agenda. While the results remain to be seen, the atmosphere is more favourable to the need for sustainable development than has been the case in the past, especially considering the peace processes in various Central American countries.

6 Lessons and challenges

One important and somewhat controversial aspect of risk-mapping is that of classifying emergency situations in the region. The difficulties relate directly to the nature and the size of the events. Hurricanes, earthquakes, and volcanic eruptions are more often seen as reasons for intervention than are phenomena such as drought, floods, and conflict. Drought and floods in particular are often recurrent, causing those affected to become victims of cyclical emergencies. Their lives permanently oscillate between stressful situations and full-blown crisis. It is therefore hard to differentiate between a 'normal' and 'emergency' state, a fact that takes us into the debate about what constitutes structural poverty and what is truly an emergency.

This risk map, particularly in its analysis of social vulnerability, proves the link between high levels of poverty and high-risk areas in the region. Not surprisingly, then, communities facing an emergency situation are at the same time living in a condition of structural poverty. If this is true in the majority of cases, does this mean that these cyclical emergencies are what bring about structural poverty?

The size of a given event and its impact are still more difficult to define if set against a global context. The differences between Mexico and Central America, Asia, and Africa are very marked, and do not readily lend themselves to comparison. It is largely agreed that emergencies that affect a given region should be understood and evaluated within that particular context, especially in terms of politics, economics, society, and culture. However, some questions arise: when exactly should an international organisation become involved in humanitarian action? What are the institutional criteria for defining an event as an emergency? What size or impact does a disaster need to have in order to produce and justify a response? Where are the dividing lines between emergency relief, rehabilitation, and reconstruction? And who decides? To aid workers on the ground, it appears that when a state of emergency is officially declared, the issues become simpler and agencies tend to intervene. However, we also know that vested political interests can prevent such a declaration being made, even when there is clearly an emergency situation. Governments also have their own definition of what constitutes an emergency, which relates to the extent to which an event will have national repercussions, although a calamitous but localised event is still an emergency for those affected by it.

How to work in disasters?

The many interviews conducted throughout this mapping exercise revealed a pattern of two opposing methods of operating in an emergency (not to mention development programmes). This is characterised by a false dichotomy between 'operational' and 'non-operational' methods, which concerns how an emergency response is formulated and put into action. On the one hand there is a tendency in some international agencies, or certain departments within them, to 'go operational' even at the expense of displacing local actors; and, on the other, some agencies adopt a position of taking no action at all unless this is done through local organisations and counterpart. The victims of this clash of viewpoints are the people affected by the calamity.

The tensions between the competing positions are heightened when top–down or head-office decisions seem to ignore or undervalue the capacity and knowledge within a given region and locally. At the same time, there is sometimes a tendency to deny the role that technical specialists may have to play. We believe, however, that this is fundamentally a false dichotomy, in that neither way of working constitutes an absolute paradigm or model. Every situation is different and requires a different combination of skills and responses. Whether a project is operational or not should be a matter of principle, but depends on a proper evaluation of each situation, and the capacity and willingness to draw on a wide repertoire of options. Where there is local, national, or regional capacity, it seems obvious that these resources should be used first, and highly specialised support would be needed only where local capacity was exceeded. There may even be 'mixed' situations where an operational presence would combine with the participation or co-ordinated action of counterparts.

Working through local organisations in emergency situations presents certain important challenges, including an assessment of whether they have the necessary expertise and capacity to respond in an appropriate fashion. There may not be local organisations through whom to work in some of the very high-risk areas. Even in areas where there are organisations already working, their capacity and scope must be weighed against the potential for an international humanitarian agency to make a wider impact. The key is to maximise any external assistance or input, while not losing sight of the need to develop local capacity.

The success of a disaster response depends largely on the capacity of the various local bodies, but this mapping exercise found that the vast majority of local organisations that are involved in development work do not focus on emergencies at all. But it is also true that they have high levels of organisational, management, and lobbying skills that could all be employed and developed in the event of an emergency.

Emergencies versus development

Where is the line drawn between emergency and rehabilitation and between rehabilitation and development? This is a critical question, in that it is common to find, even within a single institution, a complete split between what is thought of as emergency work and what is considered sustainable development. But these are not mutually exclusive: in fact, one cannot sensibly look at one without the other.

A frequent perception is that the very act of assisting in an emergency negates the concepts of sustainability and capacity-building, and that rehabilitation undermines the transformative goals of development work. In practice, emergency work does indeed mean a bigger administrative and operational workload for most people already involved in development, but it does not translate into any long-term

improvement in conditions at the community level. Given the human-resource limitations and existing workloads, this is a major reason why emergency work is not valued or is not seen as a priority.

There are real differences between development work and emergency relief. The former focuses on seeking to change the economic, social, or political systems that give rise to poverty and marginalisation. The latter focuses on preventing, mitigating, or overcoming crises that affect these systems because of the impact of a calamitous event. That is, repairing damage and rehabilitating the affected communities. Paradoxically, it is precisely these differences that reveal common ground: the complementary nature of and the continuity between the two. While development consists of a progressive process of building capacity in families and communities to satisfy needs and eventually to improve living conditions, an emergency represents a breakdown in these dynamics and even destroys the resources that do exist. At this point the communities lose the capacity to satisfy their own basic needs.

The likelihood of an emergency is ever-present. Emergencies are part of the dynamics of a community, interrupting them, slowing them down, and bringing about a complete change of direction. The risks are always foreseeable, and a true development process is responsible for controlling or minimising them.

We would argue against institutionalising a dichotomy between emergencies and development, especially given the levels of risk and vulnerability in the region. Each emergency can represent an enormous step backwards in the possibilities for development, or the disappearance of hard-earned progress in the fight against poverty. In fact, cyclical emergencies can be the cause of extreme and structural poverty. Preventing and responding to emergencies is not only a duty, it is also an imperative if efforts to promote sustainable development are to succeed in breaking this cycle.

Development programmes should incorporate a focus on disaster prevention, mitigation, and preparedness as part of their work in the field of capacity-building. Emergency programmes also need to respond to the same values, above all in ensuring that rehabilitation work supports sustainable development goals. Programmes that go beyond merely attending to damage and loss caused by calamitous events would help to resolve the immediate and long-term needs, helping to break the cycle of these events, and diminishing the need for future intervention.

Seen like this, rehabilitation is more than an opportunity for supporting the processes of sustainable development. Experience has also shown that emergency situations act as a catalyst to organisational processes such as mutual support, and could open up ways to introduce change that would otherwise be very costly in terms of resources, time, and effort. Examples have been seen in the building up of organisations and community groups, the re-valuing of the social and economic roles of women, changes in how productive or domestic activities are conducted, and so on.

Resources and finance

This way of integrating development and emergency work also presents a challenge in terms of the resources and financing required. Within the international aid industry, the marked division between emergencies and development determines funding sources and channels. Further, the agencies' thematic (sectoral) priorities make the business of implementing integral programmes in emergency situations even more complicated. It may be necessary to channel development resources towards achieving a sustainable emergency response. For example, promoting reforestation or crop diversification would help to reduce vulnerability to drought. It is also to be remembered that sustainable emergency programmes require a greater commitment, not only in terms of resources but also of time and the willingness to play an 'accompaniment' or support role with local organisations and beneficiary groups.

Conclusions

The mapping exercise confirms the high-risk conditions and great vulnerability of Mexico and Central America as a region. The scale of the damage that has been sustained in the poorest communities, as in other social and economic sectors, speaks for itself. Natural catastrophes and conflicts put brakes on development work as well as affecting the environment, the social conditions of poor people, and also the infrastructure and key

economic sectors such as agriculture and industry that are of vital importance, given the indebtedness of these countries. In addition, the social and economic conditions of the majority of people in the region are contributing to an increase in vulnerability, especially among the indigenous population and women.

The analysis of threats and risks has allowed us to identify differences between the different countries, but within a regional context in which all the countries suffer every kind of threat, from hurricanes, earthquakes, volcanic eruptions, and tsunamis to landslides and floods. And without exception all the countries are at high risk of such natural disasters. However, in carrying out a multi-phenomena analysis, we have defined those areas that are at greatest risk.

We have also established a range of needs and initiatives concerned with disaster reduction, though significant gaps exist in this area. Scientific and technical research is relatively advanced, but is often inadequate to determine local or micro-level risks. Also, vital instruments such as the cartography of phenomena are largely lacking, especially for complex sets of phenomena.

Research on vulnerability is not very developed in the region and has focused on infrastructure, rather than on the economic and social dimensions. Disaster-prevention work is intellectually weak, and not often translated into practice. Building regulations and codes exist on paper, but are seldom applied. One of the most critical aspects for the future is the absence of urban planning. The region suffers from urban sprawl, characterised by the anarchic growth of cities, and this may well get worse in years to come.

More has been achieved in the sphere of disaster preparedness for those emergencies that cannot be prevented than in the field of disaster prevention. However, improvisation is still the order of the day, as a way of managing potentially disastrous events. There are new initiatives in this area, and recently local and rural needs have been prioritised, leaving high-risk city populations to one side. Even so, the impact of plans and preparedness programmes is still very limited, and coverage is poor.

Information and training, and the evaluation of the results of research constitute the basis of the preventive and preparedness work. Here, a great deal of useful work has been done, and it is possible that the weaknesses may be overcome with the development of strong information networks on a regional and national scale.

References and background reading

Sources

Agurto, S. (1997) *Programas de Estabilización y Ajuste Estructural y sus Efectos Economicos y Sociales*, Managua: FIDEG

CONAMA (Comisión Nacional del Medio Ambiente) (1995), Plan de acción ambiental, Guatemala

Elu, M. (1996) *Maternidad Sin Riesgos en Mexico*, Mexico: Comité Promotor por una Maternidad sin Riesgos en México

Enríquez, A. (1997) *Desarrollo y ONG's en El Salvador: Retos y Perspectivas*, Revista Alternativa para el Desarrollo, 44, El Salvador

FIDEG (Fundación Internacional para el Desafio Económico Global) (1996) *La Mujer y los Hogares Rurales Nicaragüenses: Indicos Económicos y Sociales*, Managua: FIDEG

FLACSO (Facultad Latinoamericana de Ciencias Sociales) y el Instituto de la Mujer del Ministerio de Asuntos Sociales de España (1993) *Mujeres Latinoamericanas en Cifras: México*, Santiago, Chile

FLACSO (Facultad Latinoamericana de Ciencias Sociales) y el Instituto de la Mujer del Ministerio de Asuntos Sociales de España (1997) *Mujeres Latinoamericanas en Cifras: Nicaragua*, Santiago, Chile

IICA (Instituto Interamericano de Cooperación para la Agricultura)/Banco Interamericano de desarrollo (BID) (1996) *Mujeres de maiz: Programa de Análisis de la Politica del Sector Agropecuário Frente a la Mujer Productora de Alimentos en Centroamerica y Panamá*, San José, Costa Rica

INE (Instituto Nacional de Estadística), Ministerio de Salud Pública y Asistencia Social (MSPYAS), Encuestas de Demografia y Salud (DHS), USAID, UNICEF, *Encuesta Nacional de Salud Materno Infantil, 1995*, Guatemala

OPS (Organización Panamericana de la Salud) (1993) *Algunos Indicadores de Salud Seleccionados por Departamentos*, Vol. 1, Guatemala

OPS (Organización Panamericana de la Salud) (1994) *Condiciones de Salud en Guatemala*, Guatemala

OPS (Organización Panamericana de la Salud) (1996) *El Proceso de Transformación de la Salud en Guatemala*, Guatemala

Romano, E. (1996) *Represas y Desastres en El Salvador*, San Salvador: CEPRODE

UNDP (1997) *Cooperación Técnica y Financiera para El Salvador, según información proporcionada por los Cooperantes (1992-1997)*, El Salvador

In addition to the works cited here, the authors consulted a large number of unpublished reports on workshops, conference proceedings, and other regional and national events and consultation exercises.

Periodicals and other serial publications

Boletín Mensual (San Salvador): a journal about Salvadoran civil and economic affairs.

Fasículos (Mexico City): a series of monographs published in the mid-1990s on various natural phenomena, including hurricanes, tidal waves, volcanoes, and forest fires, and on factors such a chemical risks and pollution.

Revista Alternativa para el Desarrollo (San Salvador): a magazine about development alternatives. In 1997 numbers 43–47 covered topics relating to economic conditions, labour issues, and electoral developments in El Salvador.

Organisations

Organisations whose national studies and other relevant works were consulted in the course of preparing this study include the Pan-American Health Organisation of WHO, UNDP, UNICEF, and the Latin American Faculty of Social Sciences (FLACSO), based in Chile. Documents produced by the various emergencies and planning departments of the respective governments in the region were extensively consulted. Finally, the mapping exercise was enriched by the input of a large number of NGOs in Mexico and Central America, several of which are mentioned in the text

Index

Map 1: Mexico and Central America: tectonic plates, geological faults, and hurricane patterns

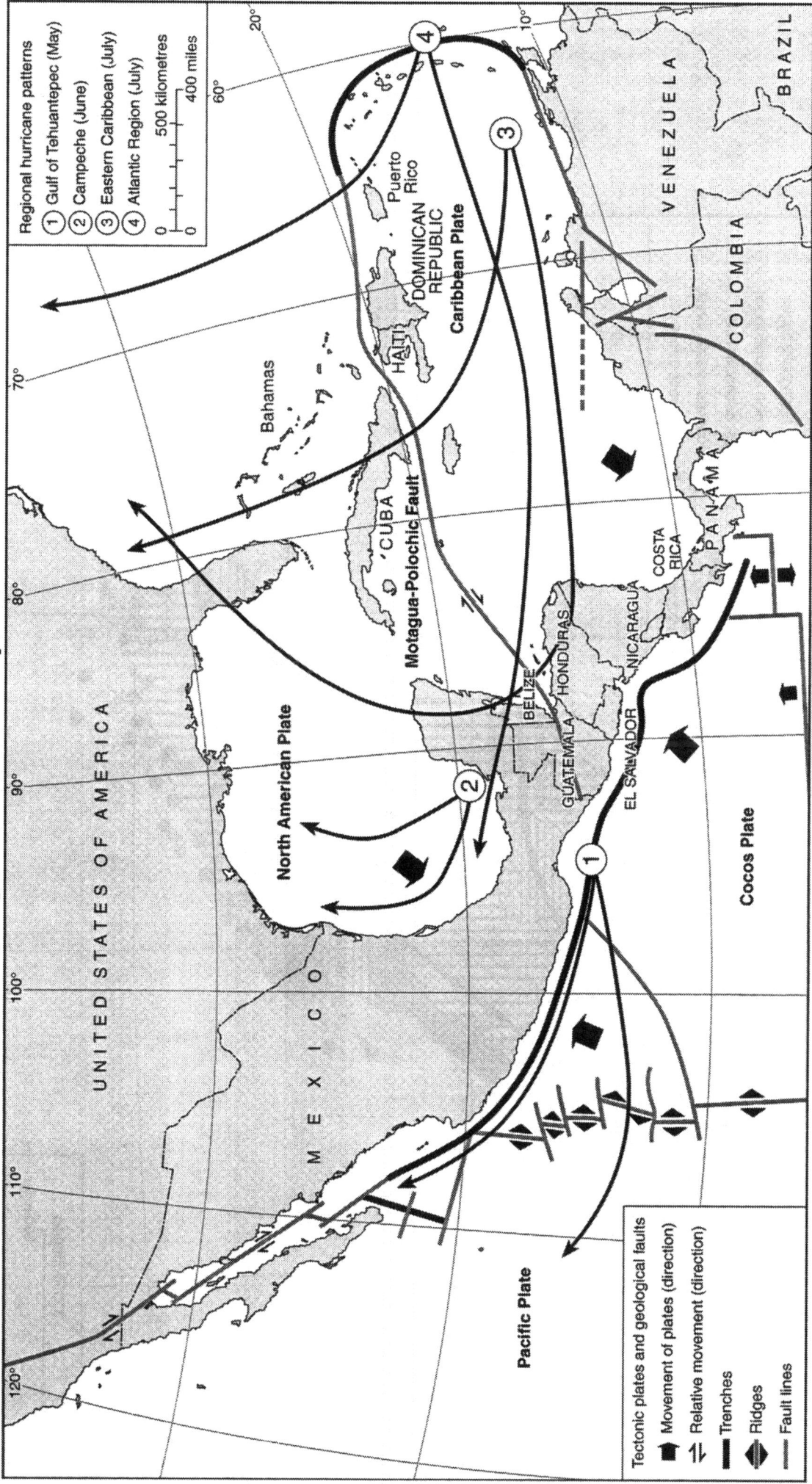

Regional hurricane patterns
① Gulf of Tehuantepec (May)
② Campeche (June)
③ Eastern Caribbean (July)
④ Atlantic Region (July)

500 kilometres
400 miles

UNITED STATES OF AMERICA

North American Plate

M E X I C O

Bahamas

'CUBA'

HAITI
DOMINICAN REPUBLIC
Puerto Rico

Caribbean Plate

Motagua-Polochic Fault

BELIZE
GUATEMALA
HONDURAS
EL SALVADOR
NICARAGUA
COSTA RICA
PANAMÁ

VENEZUELA

COLOMBIA

BRAZIL

Pacific Plate

Cocos Plate

Tectonic plates and geological faults
◆ Movement of plates (direction)
⇅ Relative movement (direction)
▮ Trenches
◆ Ridges
— Fault lines

map 1

Map 2: Mexico: natural risks and vulnerability

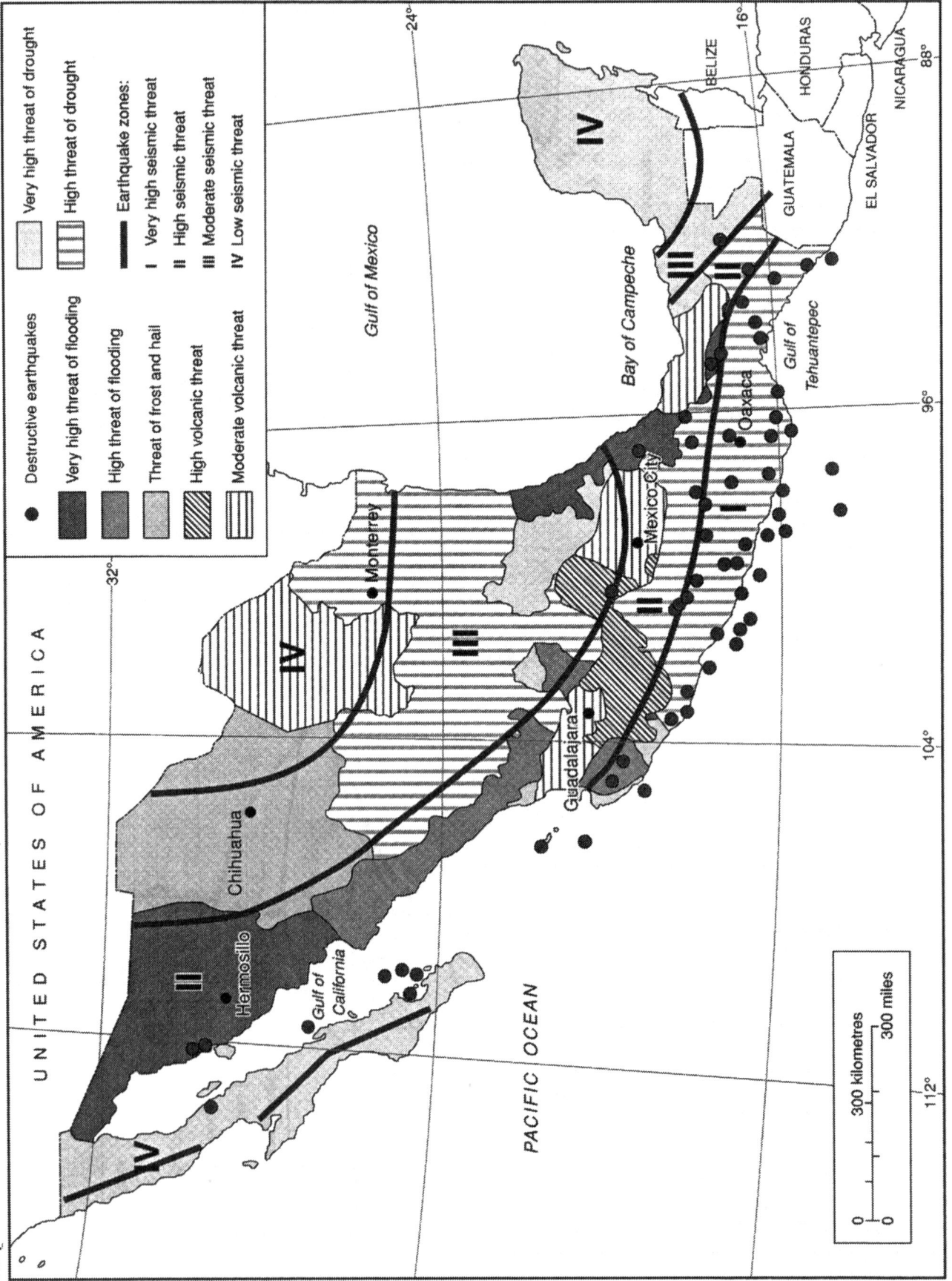

Legend:

Destructive earthquakes •

- Very high threat of flooding
- High threat of flooding
- Threat of frost and hail
- High volcanic threat
- Moderate volcanic threat

- Very high threat of drought
- High threat of drought

Earthquake zones:
- Very high seismic threat
- I High seismic threat
- II Moderate seismic threat
- III
- IV Low seismic threat

UNITED STATES OF AMERICA

Hermosillo
Chihuahua
Monterrey
Guadalajara
Mexico City
Oaxaca

Gulf of California
PACIFIC OCEAN
Gulf of Mexico
Bay of Campeche
Gulf of Tehuantepec

BELIZE
GUATEMALA
HONDURAS
EL SALVADOR
NICARAGUA

0   300 kilometres
0   300 miles

32°   24°   16°
112°   104°   96°   88°

Map 3: Central America: risks of earthquakes and volcanic activity

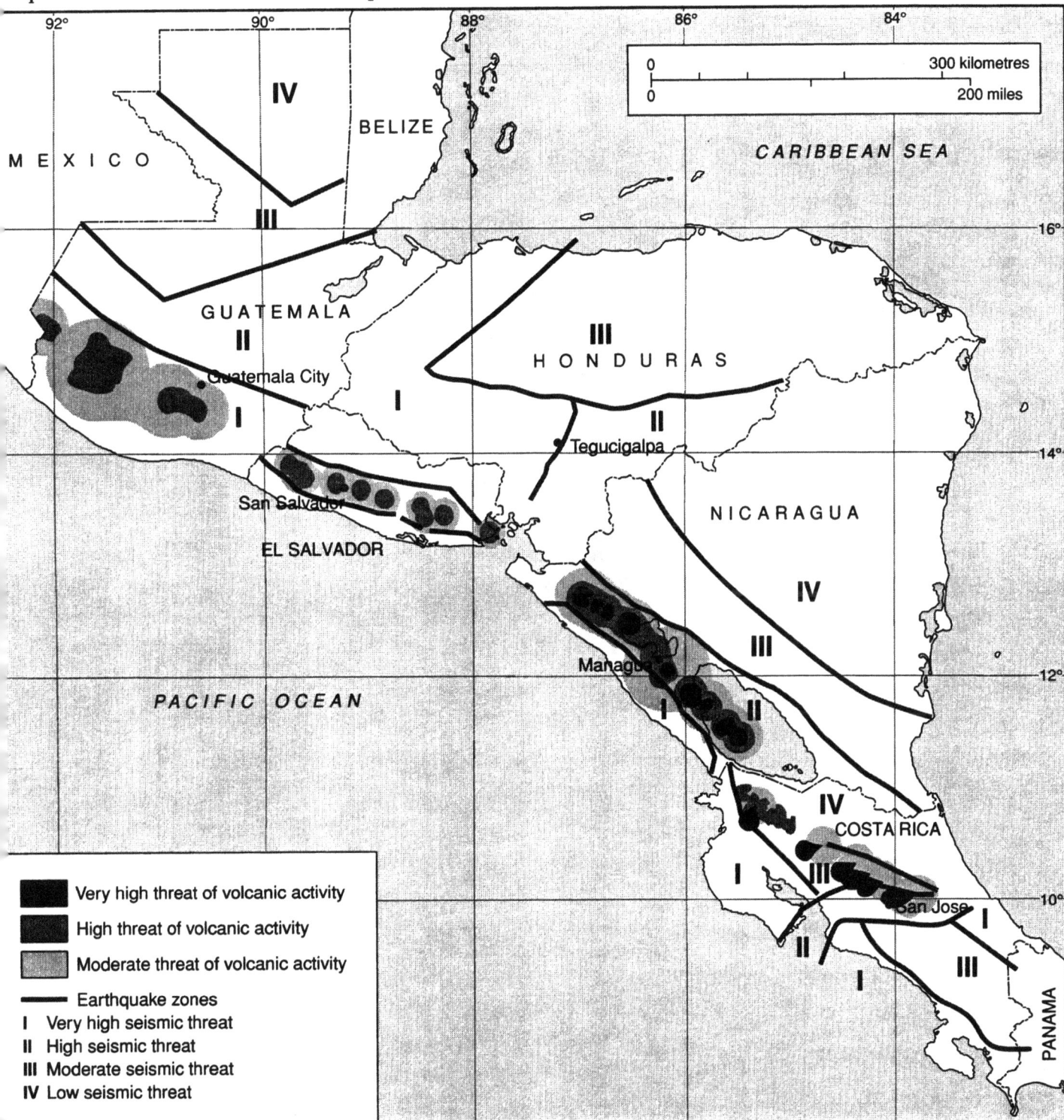

MEXICO

BELIZE

CARIBBEAN SEA

0   300 kilometres

0   200 miles

IV

III

GUATEMALA

II

Guatemala City

I

HONDURAS

III

I

Tegucigalpa

II

NICARAGUA

San Salvador

EL SALVADOR

IV

III

PACIFIC OCEAN

Managua

I

II

IV

COSTA RICA

I

III

San Jose

I

II

III

I

PANAMA

Very high threat of volcanic activity

High threat of volcanic activity

Moderate threat of volcanic activity

Earthquake zones
I   Very high seismic threat
II   High seismic threat
III   Moderate seismic threat
IV   Low seismic threat

92°   90°   88°   86°   84°

16°

14°

12°

10°

Map 4: Central America: risks of floods, landslides, and drought

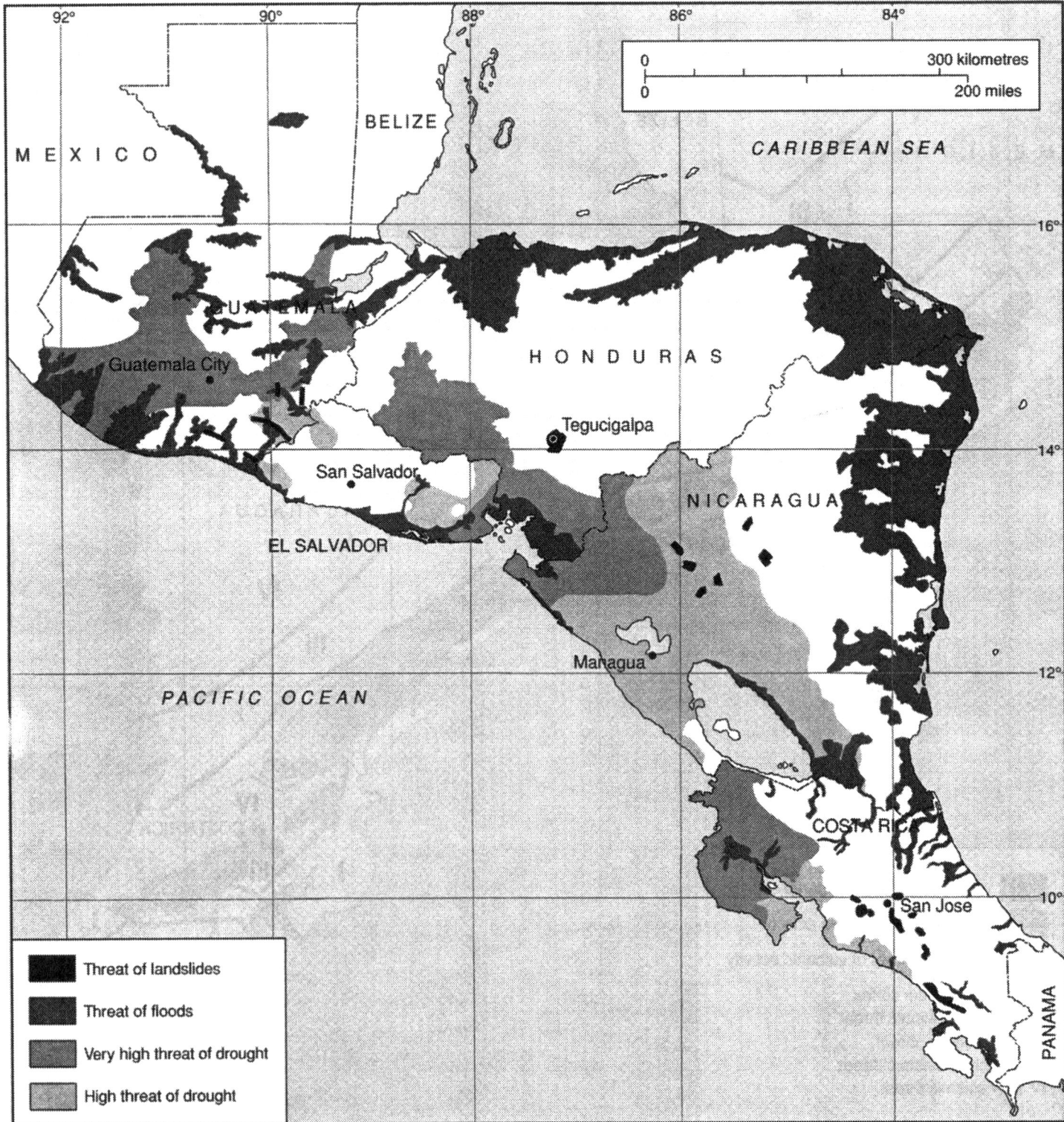

0	300 kilometres
0	200 miles

MEXICO

BELIZE

CARIBBEAN SEA

GUATEMALA

Guatemala City

HONDURAS

Tegucigalpa

San Salvador

EL SALVADOR

NICARAGUA

PACIFIC OCEAN

Managua

COSTA RICA

San Jose

PANAMA

- ■ Threat of landslides
- ■ Threat of floods
- ■ Very high threat of drought
- ■ High threat of drought